Developing
Community-
Empowered
Schools

Developing

Community-Empowered Schools

Mary Ann Burke
Lawrence O. Picus

CORWIN PRESS, INC.
A Sage Publications Company
Thousand Oaks, California

For information:

Corwin Press, Inc.
A Sage Publications Company
2455 Teller Road
Thousand Oaks, California 91320
E-mail: order@corwinpress.com

Sage Publications Ltd.
6 Bonhill Street
London EC2A 4PU
United Kingdom

Sage Publications India Pvt. Ltd.
M-32 Market
Greater Kailash I
New Delhi 110 048 India

Printed in the United States of America

Library of Congress Cataloging-in-Publication Data

Burke, Mary Ann.
    Developing community-empowered schools / by Mary Ann Burke and
Lawrence O. Picus; with the Fenton Avenue Charter School Staff.
        p. cm.
    Includes bibliographical references and index.
    ISBN 0-7619-7789-9 (c) — ISBN 0-7619-7790-2 (p)
    1. Community and school. 2. School improvement programs. I. Picus,
Larry, 1954– . II. Fenton Avenue Charter School (Lake View Terrace,
Calif.) III. Title.
    LC215 .B78 2000
    371.19—dc21   00-012044

This book is printed on acid-free paper.

01 02 03 04 05 06 07 7 6 5 4 3 2 1

Acquiring Editor:	Robb Clouse
Editorial Assistant:	Kylee Liegl
Production Editor:	Diane S. Foster
Editorial Assistant:	Cindy Bear
Typesetter/Designer:	Lynn Miyata
Cover Designer:	Michelle Lee

Contents

CORWIN PRESS

The Corwin Press logo—a raven striding across an open book—represents the happy union of courage and learning. We are a professional-level publisher of books and journals for K–12 educators, and we are committed to creating and providing resources that embody these qualities. Corwin's motto is "Success for All Learners."

Acknowledgments

■ ■

Our purpose in writing this book is to share the knowledge we have gained throughout our years of working with school communities to increase parent and community involvement with others throughout the country. We strongly believe that by empowering the stakeholders at each school site, better decisions about educational programs that will improve learning for all students will result. The sample training materials presented in this book were designed over many years of work and represent examples that we have found to be successful. None of this could have been accomplished without the hard work and dedication of many other people in a wide range of schools and school districts.

We are indebted to many individuals who have assisted us throughout our years of research. We thank Diana Marich, Parent Educator Coordinator of the Parent Education Preschool Program at the Sunnyvale/Cupertino Adult Education Center, who has provided extensive support and guidance in creating innovative parent and community education programs for nearly 20 years. Dr. Terry Johnston, Dr. Lee Mahon, and Dr. Mitsu Kumagai have served as mentors for more than a decade in developing effective strategies for building school-linked community partnerships. Carl Liljenstolpe continues to provide staff development and sales automation and marketing training in assisting community-based organizations to partner with schools.

Dr. Reynaldo Baca from the Center for Multilingual, Multicultural Research in the Rossier School of Education at the University of Southern California continues to serve as our social conscience in developing equitable school programs for culturally diverse populations. Professor William B. Michael from the Division of Educational Psychology and Technology in the Rossier School of Education at the University of Southern California has helped us create alternative assessment instruments for measuring the impact of these partnership programs on students' academic performance. Professor Stuart Gothold from the Rossier School of Education at the University of Southern California continues to provide transformational leadership support in forming new school and community collaborative partnerships.

Fenton Avenue Charter School's administrators, teachers, and staff spent hundreds of hours designing, piloting, and modifying the school, family, and community partnership training materials to support its parent and community volunteer program. Appreciation goes to Dr. Magaly Lavadenz from Loyola Marymount University, Rossier School of Education Dean Guilbert C. Hentschke, and Rossier School of Education Professional Studies Manager Jeffrey Davis for sponsoring and coordinating the continuing education program component. Special thanks to Gayle Hawkins, our Corporation for National Service State Program Specialist, and to our AmeriCorps VISTA members for their diligence and courageous commitment in assisting us with recruiting and training the parent and community volunteers to serve as classroom mentors and tutors.

We would not have been able to complete the ongoing research for this project without the commitment and sponsorship from Compton Unified School District. Special thanks to Accountability Officer Cathy Jones, Compliance Administrator Tom Brown, State Administrator Dr. Randolph Ward, and former Deputy Superintendent Dr. George J. McKenna, III, who have continued to work with us in creating and piloting unique school- and community-based partnerships using Epstein's framework of six types of involvement.

Finally, heart-felt thanks goes to all of our families, who have made countless sacrifices for us to pursue our passionate dream of providing culturally and economically diverse families with the necessary tools to support their children's academic success.

About the Authors

■ ■

Mary Ann Burke, EdD, is Adjunct Assistant Professor in the Rossier School of Education at the University of Southern California, where she specializes in resource development for education. She is also Grants and Assessment Administrator for Compton Unified School District and assists the district's schools in building partnerships with parents and community volunteers for school site services and resource development. She is the former director of the Community Partnership Coalition VISTA Project sponsored by Fenton Avenue Charter School. The project recruits and trains parents and community volunteers to serve as mentors and tutors in the classroom. She is coauthor of *Recruiting Volunteers* and *Creative Fundraising.*

Lawrence O. Picus, PhD, is Professor and Chair of the Department of Administration and Policy in the Rossier School of Education at the University of Southern California. He also serves as Director of the Center for Research in Education Finance (CREF), a school finance research center housed at the Rossier School of Education. CREF research focuses on issues of school finance and productivity. His current research interests focus on adequacy and equity in school finance as well as efficiency and productivity in the provision of educational programs for kindergarten through 12th-grade schoolchildren. He is coauthor (with Allan Odden) of *School Finance: A Policy Perspective,* 2nd ed. (McGraw-Hill, 2000) and (with R. Craig Wood, David Thompson, and Don I. Tharpe) *Principles of School Business Administration* (ASBO, 1995). In addition, he was the senior editor of the 1995 yearbook of the American Education Finance Association, *Where Does the Money Go? Resource Allocation in Elementary and Secondary Schools* (Corwin Press, 1995). In his role with CREF, he is involved with studies of how educational resources are allocated and used in schools throughout the United States. He maintains close contact with the superintendents and chief business officers of school districts throughout California and the nation, and he is a member of many professional organizations dedicated to improving school district management. He is a former member of the Editorial Advisory Committee of the Association of School Business Officials, International, and he has served as a consultant to the National Education Association, American

Federation of Teachers, the National Center for Education Statistics, WestEd, and the states of Washington, Vermont, Oregon, Wyoming, South Carolina, Louisiana, and Arkansas.

Fenton Avenue Charter School's former assistant director, Yvette King-Berg, and classroom teachers Jennifer Nishimoto, Ana Luisa Wolfer, and Donald Ausherman designed, piloted, and modified the school, family, and community partnership training materials for school site teachers, administrators, parents, and community volunteers. The California Distinguished School is the largest urban kindergarten through fifth-grade public elementary charter school in the United States and is located in the San Fernando Valley. The year-round, multitrack school currently serves 1,340 primarily low-income students of racially, culturally, and linguistically diverse backgrounds. Fenton provides a model of successful training and implementation strategies for using parents and community volunteers to support classroom activities and the school's governance.

Introduction

■ ■

The value of parent and community volunteers working with students to support their academic performance has received increasing attention. This book describes many effective strategies that we have developed working with these stakeholders at school sites during the past 20 years. While teaching parents about child development concerns, we found that parents not only needed to understand how to respond to their child's age-appropriate behavior but also were eager to learn ways to effectively work in partnership with their child's school (Burke, 1999).

In our research, we discovered that many parents were not aware of their legal rights for accessing appropriate services to support their child's learning or how they could request testing when their child was failing in school. The right for an equitable education was jeopardized for parents and students of low-income families, who had limited access to resources to support the students' success in school. Non-native English-speaking and limited English-speaking parents were further challenged in trying to learn how the school system in the United States differed from those of their homelands. We found that many teachers—in response to the diverse needs of students and their parents—have become social service resources helping families learn to access school and community services.

The Value of Family Centers

In recent years, many schools have responded to the diverse needs of families by creating on-site parent centers. These centers provide parent education classes, English as a second language classes, basic subject classes, computer literacy job training classes, and classes on how parents can help their children learn at home. Through government-funded initiatives (e.g., Healthy Start), families and community members are able to support school site administrators, teachers, and staff in planning, identifying, and providing appropriate academic services to diverse student groups. Many independently governed and fiscally autonomous public charter schools have created their own nonprofit family centers, often with state or federal support or both. These centers are governed by boards of directors and provide social services to families in the communities. These centers can contribute to the economic sustainability of the community, and they are often a source of parent and community volunteers in the schools.

Concerns About Parent and Community Involvement

On the surface, the use of parent and community volunteers to help in classrooms seems valuable. Administrators and teachers have raised many legitimate concerns, however, that must be addressed to successfully implement school, family, and community partnership programs. Administrative concerns identified in our research include the following (Burke, 1999):

- Management of parent, school, and community partnership programs to ensure that students will be safe and secure at the school site

- Anxiety about providing parents with too much knowledge about their rights to ensure an equitable education for their child, and a fear that parents would demand too many costly services to ensure their child's academic success

- Fear of losing control over provision of a quality school education in the school

Teacher concerns included the following (Burke, 1999):

- Anxiety regarding having parents and community volunteers work in the classroom with students

- Fear of criticism about teaching style or methods

- Concern about the impact of volunteer use of improper English on student learning

- Concern that volunteers would not have an adequate understanding of appropriate student behaviors, effective teaching strategies, and ways to nurture a student's academic success

We also found that parents and community members who volunteered in the schools had a substantial need for additional training and information, including the following (Burke, 1999):

- How to access academic support services

- How to help their children become successful in school

■ A deeper understanding of effective strategies for helping their children complete homework

■ More information about what they should do when their children were confused about homework and when their children expressed indifference about school

■ Training on effective strategies for promoting literacy

■ Greater knowledge of age-appropriate behaviors and expectations of students

■ Information about how to work with the school to create additional student support programs and resources for the school

Epstein's Framework

We found Epstein's 6-point framework for parent and community involvement to be helpful in addressing these needs (Epstein, Coates, Salinas, Sanders, & Simon, 1997). Epstein et al. postulate six types of parent and community involvement in schools that help educators develop more comprehensive partnerships with the school and family through program development and that help schools and researchers evaluate the results of these various levels of involvement.

Type 1 is the parenting level of involvement. It is designed to provide families with training in how to establish a supportive home environment for student learning. Activities that are supportive of Type 1 involvement include home visits by school personnel, child-rearing workshops, and computerized messages from the school on parent education topics. It can also include support programs to assist families with health, nutrition, and other social services.

Type 2 is the communicating level of involvement. Activities at this level include parent-teacher conferences, language translation services, and weekly folder transmittals to parents with students' work, classroom newsletters, and informational pieces describing the school procedures and policies.

Activities to support a school's Type 3, or volunteering level of involvement, include volunteer recruitment and training activities required to adequately prepare parent and community volunteers to assist in the classroom and provide schoolwide administrative support.

Type 4 is the learning at home level of involvement. Activities at this level include providing parents with information on the skills required for student success at each grade and teaching parents how to help students with their homework.

Type 5 is the decision-making level of involvement. Type 5 activities include recruiting parent and community volunteers to serve as decision-making school leaders and representatives.

Collaborating with the community is Epstein's Type 6 level of involvement. At this advanced level, school involvement activities include integrating community partnerships, resources, and services into a school's daily programs. School partnerships can be built with community agencies, governmental entities, businesses, and alumni groups.

Parent and Community Training

To prepare school site administrators and teachers for developing the previously discussed levels of parent and community involvement, we designed a series of training sessions for skill development. Each session focused on how parent and community volunteers could be organized to adequately support teachers and school site administrators in managing school operations and in providing academic support to students in the classroom. Since the initial pilot of these training sessions at Fenton Avenue Charter School in 1998, we have developed additional training programs that focus on how to support schools' service learning activities and how school districts can formulate parent participation and community involvement policies and procedures. Our recent work includes providing technical support to the Compton Unified School District and Los Angeles County charter schools in creating a comprehensive array of programs using Epstein's six types of involvement activities. Schools that include all these forms of parent involvement help parents build home conditions that can support their children's learning (Lewis, 1992). This book describes the training sessions, provides the rationale for each training component, and offers sample materials others can use to train parents and other community volunteers in their own school community.

There is ample evidence that parental and community involvement can positively influence students' academic success, regardless of a family's income or education (Funkhouser, Gonzales, & Moles, 1998; Henderson & Berla, 1994; Karnes, 1979; Young & Westernoff, 1996). Since the 1960s, the majority of state and federally funded programs have included a parent and community participation component. Project Head Start and Title I are examples of federal programs with such a requirement.

The impact of parent and community involvement in schools cannot be overemphasized. From the time a child is born, parents are a child's first teachers (Henderson, Marburger, & Ooms, 1986). They teach their child how to eat, speak, take care of himself or herself, and play with other children. Although it is the school's job to teach their child how to read and write, it is the parents' responsibility to show their child that school is important and homework must be finished (Far West Laboratory, 1992; White, 1987). Parents need to stay informed of their child's progress in school, take advantage of school services, meet with teachers on a regular basis, actively participate in teacher-parent conferences, and support teachers' professional growth (Dodd, 1992). When a parent does not have the skills to support the school and help his or her child with homework, it is the school's responsibility to support the parent in learning how to help his or her child. When parents are unavailable or unable to help their child succeed in school, community mentors can provide the necessary support.

Research has indicated that students do well in school when their parents express high expectations for school achievement and provide support in their student's learning (Young & Westernoff, 1996). To overcome traditional communication barriers, schools must provide parents and community volunteers with adequate information for making appropriate educational decisions to support each student's academic success.

Teachers working with families of differing cultures must be sensitive to the cultural interpretations and different perceptions of the educational system and to their roles with parents (Young & Westernoff, 1996). Parents from varying cultures may initially interpret the educational system based on their own cultural experiences. Parents' cultural sensitivity about the importance of education and the teacher's understanding about educational systems in other countries can help build effective partnerships (Young & Westernoff, 1996). Awareness of one's cultural behaviors, beliefs, and values is critical to forming effective parent and teacher relationships. This awareness can be generated by acknowledging different cultural perspectives and by gathering information about the students' cultures. Increased parent participation can be encouraged at schools by recognizing that parents are valuable multicultural resources. As multicultural resources, parents can speak on culturally relevant topics, participate in international events, and translate parent education materials.

Organization of the Book

The eight chapters in this book develop an effective approach for implementing successful school, family, and community partnership activities.

Chapter 1 examines the components of a community-empowered school, which include orderly facilities, friendly staff members, adequate support services, and a comprehensive volunteer and resource development plan.

Chapter 2 identifies the stakeholders in a school and defines the role of each stakeholder, describing what each can do to support a community-empowered school in reaching its academic and resource development goals.

Chapter 3 describes the policies and procedures that support school and community relationships, including program monitoring, supervision, and volunteer support policies.

Chapter 4 provides overheads and training worksheets to support a 1-day teacher-training workshop on the use of parent or community tutors and mentors in the classroom. The sample training materials include examples of program policies and procedures as well as materials to help both volunteers and teachers understand their respective roles in a community-empowered school. In addition, sample memos from teachers to students' families are included to help teachers implement a program such as the one we describe.

Chapter 5 identifies effective volunteer strategies that support school-based family and student literacy activities in reading, writing, math, science, social studies, computer technology, and the performing arts.

Chapter 6 describes how schools can build successful community problem-solving collaborative projects with the community's stakeholders. It also provides an overview of how to seek grant funding to sustain a school-based community program.

Chapter 7 explains how using the community as a school's resource can provide a cost-effective solution to school finance problems. The advantages of a cost-benefit analysis, a cost utility analysis, and the production function for effective community resource planning and utilization are discussed.

Chapter 8 describes the roles of various community stakeholders in formulating public policies that support a school's role as a resource that can contribute to its community's economy.

What Is a Community-Empowered School?

■ ■

A *community-empowered school* is one in which all members of the community—administrators, teachers, school staff, students, parents, and members of the local community at large—participate in efforts to achieve a school's goal of improving student performance. Schools that promote empowerment of all these stakeholders often emphasize shared decision making. This participation tends to make schools more effective in reaching learning goals and can improve the overall satisfaction of the stakeholders in their participation in school activities (Short & Greer, 1997).

Establishing and maintaining a community-empowered school requires dedication and hard work. To encourage shared decision making and to reward risk taking and innovation, school leadership in a community-empowered school must provide opportunities for professional development for all of the school's stakeholders. By providing stakeholders with ongoing support, a school's administration can help the entire community work toward the goal of academic success for all students. To establish an environment of trust in a school, administrators' and teachers' attitudinal predisposition toward caring for individual students needs to be overtly conveyed and confirmed in relationships with the various stakeholders (Valenzuela, 1999).

Characteristics of a Community-Empowered School

In the following sections, characteristics that we have observed over time in a wide range of community-empowered schools are discussed. We believe that these characteristics can effectively nurture the academic success of culturally and economically diverse student populations.

A Clean and Orderly Facility

First impressions are vital for building the trust and respect of various community stakeholders. The condition of a facility reflects the way business is conducted at a school site. When a school is clean, orderly, and well maintained, community stakeholders can anticipate that the students will be supported in the same way. If the school does not convey a sense of security and orderliness to parents, the school's administrators will be challenged to gain the trust of parents in its delivery of services. A school's "pride of ownership" can also be displayed through its mission statement, by the information provided to visitors on announcement signs, and on its front office bulletin boards. A community-empowered school can display the names of key community leaders who have visited the school on bulletin boards in addition to the names of a featured teacher and volunteer of the month. A school's displayed mission statement can include the roles for various stakeholders in supporting students' academic success.

Classrooms should be orderly and reflect a teacher's individual teaching style in relation to the curriculum being presented to students. This includes the information provided on classroom bulletin boards, student work displayed in the classroom, the overall organization of the classroom, and the classroom layout.

A Friendly Staff With Effective Communication Support Services

When parents, students, and community members arrive at a school, a favorable first impression is important and will impact the individual's view of the school to a considerable extent. Consequently, the way visitors are greeted and then treated by staff members is a critical component (Henderson, Marburger, & Ooms, 1986). When a visitor is treated in a courteous, attentive, and respectful way, the visitor will immediately feel more relaxed and can trust that his or her needs are important and will be sufficiently addressed. Due to the English language limitations of visitors in some school districts, schools increasingly face the challenge of adequately communicating their policies and procedures to linguistically diverse community stakeholders. How a school responds to this critical need is vital for building effective school, parent, and community relationships. How school staff respond to non-English-speaking visitors is an important consideration. Translators, who can speak the languages of the community's students, should be available to assist parents and community members. These translators should be able to fully translate a visitor's concerns and issues to the appropriate administrators.

Once a parent or community member arrives at the school, it is important for the school's staff to assess the visitor's need and identify the appropriate person who can best respond to that need. A school can display an organizational chart indicating the roles and responsibilities of various school administrators and support staff for parent and community volunteers to contact. The school should also have a list of translators available to support the language needs of its culturally diverse community.

Community-empowered schools should have all of their policies and procedures clearly articulated in a parent and community handbook. The handbook should be updated at the beginning of each year. During the school year, a weekly bulletin can be sent home to parents highlighting upcoming meetings and school activities. Monthly or bimonthly school newspapers with critical information about the school's activities and services can be mailed to parents and interested community members. In addition, accomplishments of the school and its students should be featured in each publication.

All school communication pieces should highlight the various school services and explain how parents and community members can access those services. The names and phone numbers of administrators and support staff to contact for each service need to be listed along with a sample of the services provided within a program. The days and times for each service should be included. If it is necessary to register for a service provided by the school, it is important to clearly describe the registration process and how parents, students, or community members can register. All information communicated to parents and various community stakeholders should be translated and distributed in the primary languages spoken within the community. With clear communication, parents and community stakeholders can best respond to the diverse needs of their students and assist them in maximizing their academic achievement.

A School's Support Services Outside of the Classroom

As the needs of students have increased in the past decade, community-empowered schools have created a multitude of support services to respond to these needs. The demands for these services are extensive. There are more single-parent homes, more two-income households, increased cultural and linguistic diversity, greater income disparity among community members, and increasing demand for safe and secure schools. To address these emerging needs, community-empowered schools are partnering with other community agencies (public and private) to provide a more coordinated delivery of health care services. Such coordinated services are expected to help improve students' chances for success.

Depending on the needs of the school community, a school may provide a case management approach to addressing individual student concerns by referring the student and his or her family to appropriate health care and social services agencies for assistance. In other cases, a community-empowered school might partner with health care and social services agencies to provide services directly on campus. Some community-empowered schools have had success using a parent center to help with the coordination and provision of comprehensive services for children. The following is a sample of the various services that community-empowered schools are currently providing at school sites or through referrals or both (Burke, 1999; Epstein, Coates, Salinas, Sanders, & Simon, 1997):

- Parent education training workshops presented by the school's teachers on how parents can support their children's academic success; these workshops emphasize the actual curriculum being used in the classroom

- After-school academic tutorial support services for students and their families

- Cultural and community enrichment fairs and events

- Literacy activities provided at the school site in partnership with the local library

- Saturday and evening family literacy and academic enrichment programs

- Family math and bedtime reading programs

- Parent education classes relating to child development issues and how parents can adequately support their children in school

- Job training and skill-building courses, including English as a second language classes, basic math, computer literacy training, and career development guidance

- A comprehensive special education service delivery system

- Social services and referrals, including case management, health fairs through mobile health care clinics, hearing screening, vision exams, on-site immunization clinics, nutritional food distribution programs, mental health counseling intervention and prevention services, child care services, and after-school and weekend youth development programs

A Comprehensive Volunteer and Resource Development Program

When a parent or community visitor approaches a school about volunteer opportunities or how to provide resources, a community-empowered school must have a clear process in place regarding how a parent or community volunteer can support the school. How a school responds to a volunteer's offer of assistance, while maintaining its academic integrity and safety for its students, has received increased attention in recent years. The delicate balance of establishing policies and procedures to ensure students' safety and academic program quality can be challenged when the merits of actively engaging parents and community volunteers are considered. When a school can adequately train and support its teachers, parents, and community volunteers to cooperatively support students as effective partners, parent and community involvement can have a significant impact on students' overall academic performance and the overall community's support of the school (Aronson, 1995). Community-empowered schools can respond to this challenge by involving all stakeholders in their governance and program delivery.

Assessing Your School's Strengths and Weaknesses

The first step in developing a community-empowered school is to assess the strengths and weaknesses of your community for building effective partnerships. Figure 1.1 contains a draft assessment form that you can use to conduct such an assessment. Review and complete this assessment to identify your school's strengths and weaknesses in building effective partnerships with your family and school community. Chapter 2 provides a discussion of who should be included as a school's stakeholders. Chapter 3 identifies the types of policies and procedures that can support effective school, family, and community partnerships.

FIGURE 1.1. Sample Instrument for Assessing Your School's Potential for Building Effective Family and Community Partnerships

Consider the following characteristics at your school, and circle the appropriate numerical value (1 = high and 5 = low) to rate your school's potential for building partnerships:

	High			**Low**	
1. The school's location in the community	1	2	3	4	5
2. The overall appearance of the facility	1	2	3	4	5
3. The school's announcement board and signage	1	2	3	4	5
4. The appearance and organization of the front office	1	2	3	4	5
5. The front office's information and bulletin boards	1	2	3	4	5
6. The front office display of key community visitors	1	2	3	4	5
7. The front office monthly display of a featured teacher and volunteer	1	2	3	4	5
8. The school's mission displayed in the front office	1	2	3	4	5
9. Orderly classrooms that reflect the teacher's curriculum and style	1	2	3	4	5
10. Students' work displayed in classrooms and throughout the school	1	2	3	4	5
11. The overall classroom layout	1	2	3	4	5
12. How parents and visitors are greeted at the front office	1	2	3	4	5
13. The availability of translation services for limited English speakers	1	2	3	4	5
14. A clear understanding of who should support various visitor needs	1	2	3	4	5
15. A list of translators available to support various translation needs	1	2	3	4	5
16. A parent and community handbook outlining the school's policies	1	2	3	4	5
17. A weekly bulletin highlighting upcoming meetings and activities	1	2	3	4	5
18. Monthly or bimonthly school newspapers	1	2	3	4	5
19. A listing of each program's contact name and phone number	1	2	3	4	5
20. Clear communication materials for parents and the community	1	2	3	4	5

	High			Low	
21. Adequate academic support services for students and families	1	2	3	4	5
22. Adequate health and human care referral services for families	1	2	3	4	5
23. Adequate health and human care services at the school site	1	2	3	4	5
24. Sufficient community-based partnerships for services	1	2	3	4	5
25. Sufficient community partnerships with all stakeholders	1	2	3	4	5
26. Sufficient child care programs at the school site	1	2	3	4	5
27. A clear process for volunteer development and donations	1	2	3	4	5
28. School policies and procedures that ensure student safety	1	2	3	4	5
29. School policies for volunteers to support students' achievement	1	2	3	4	5
30. Sufficient volunteer use of staff development training	1	2	3	4	5
31. Sufficient parent and community volunteer training	1	2	3	4	5
32. Effective partnerships with parents, families, and the community	1	2	3	4	5

List your school's three strongest characteristics that support partnership development:

1. _____

2. _____

3. _____

List three strategies that would strengthen your school's ability to build effective partnerships with various stakeholder groups:

1. _____

2. _____

3. _____

CHAPTER

Who Are the Stakeholders?

■ ■

A school community consists of students, school site administrators, program support and clerical staff, teachers, parents, community volunteers, community-based agencies, local businesses, district personnel, legislators, governmental agencies, and funders. How a school communicates with these various stakeholders will establish its community's ability to build critical and effective partnerships that can ensure students' overall academic success and the ability to access services and resources (Schmitt & Tracy, 1996). This chapter provides a summary of various stakeholders' roles and outlines how each group can support a community-empowered school in achieving its academic and resource development goals.

Teachers

A school's teachers are responsible for providing students with appropriate grade-level instruction, curriculum, and academic guidance. The classroom teacher is the critical link to a student's academic success. How a teacher relates to individual students and their parents is critical for building a supportive and nurturing environment for students' academic success (Schmitt & Tracy, 1996). When a teacher suspects that a student needs additional support to attain academic success, it is the teacher's responsibility to contact appropriate support staff and the student's parents to accommodate that child's unique learning style.

Unfortunately, most teacher preparation programs provide only limited training to teachers in how to approach, educate, and support parents and community volunteers. Many teachers feel anxious and overwhelmed when meeting parents and community members at back-to-school nights and at parent-teacher conferences. To prepare for these events, teachers can provide parents with handouts and a brief overview of the curriculum offerings and classroom procedures. Few teachers feel qualified to teach parents to support their children in homework and skill acquisition. Fewer teachers are confident that parents can adequately provide such academic support for their children. This concern is greater when the parents are not proficient in English or when parents have a limited educational background.

School Site Administrators

School administrators include all staff members who are responsible for supervising the overall daily operations of a school: the principal, assistant principal, project coordinators, and directors. How the school administrators relate to parents and the greater school community can create an environment that will nurture trust among all stakeholders. It is vital for the school site administrators, along with other stakeholders, to create schoolwide policies and procedures that will provide an adequate balance of structure and freedom for developing comprehensive schoolwide community partnership programs.

Program Support and Clerical Staff

All staff providing program and overall administrative support are included in this category. The school office employees are typically the first point of contact for parents and community members visiting the school. If these individuals show genuine interest in the concerns and needs of parents, students, and community members, it will set the right tone for further encounters with other school staff, including administrators and teachers.

Parents

As the first and primary teachers of their children, parents are a critical component in their children's academic success. Regardless of parents' previous academic experiences, parents can be trained and mentored in effective strategies to support their children's learning. Once parents have received this training and are more comfortable working with their own children, many choose to increase their own academic skills to benefit both their children and themselves. Well-informed parents can help their children with homework. They can also serve as parent volunteers in the classroom supporting the educational needs of their children and their children's peers. Empowered and well-informed parents are often active supporters of their school's administration, working to help solve problems, make policy, or raise additional funds for the school.

Community Volunteers

When a student does not have a parent available to support his or her academic needs, community volunteers can be instrumental in providing academic mentorship and assistance. Community volunteers include students from other grades, college students, community members, grandparents, parents of children in other grade levels, and employees from local companies. To successfully use community volunteers, it is important for a school to have appropriate policies and procedures that support community volunteer programs.

Community-Based Organizations

Community-based organizations can provide a school with volunteers, funding resources, and a range of health and human care services that support students and their families. A school can be the primary neighborhood provider for a multitude of community-based services for all students and their families. These services include counseling; prevention, intervention, and referral services; parent education classes; employment development courses; family literacy programs; library services; basic needs services; case management support services; child and adult day care; senior care referral services; legal and immigration assistance; and medical and dental services and referrals. School site administrators need to establish community partnership policies that determine how a school will enlist program support from community-based organizations.

Local Businesses

Local businesses are often a good source of support for public schools. Local businesses can provide volunteer services and resources to neighborhood schools. Many companies donate computers, telecommunications equipment, office furniture and machines, and other capital equipment. Donated business services include installing computers and computer network systems, providing staff development training, donating duplicating services and art materials, and sponsoring events. Businesses can provide employee volunteers to assist in the classroom and provide technical support in the school's daily operations. Companies that provide this assistance believe that supporting their local schools makes good business sense.

District Personnel

Although the focus of this book is on the school site, the importance of support from the district office cannot be ignored. Regardless of the level of true site-based decision making in a district, the distribution of most funds to a school site is determined at the district level. Moreover, schools rely on central office staff to provide personnel services, support for major repairs and renovations, and general budget support. Maintaining a strong and congenial relationship with the central office makes the general operation of any school site more efficient. Moreover, the central office has a stake in the academic success of all students in a district and therefore is highly invested in the success of individual schools. The first step in taking successful community-empowerment models to scale is to implement the successful ideas from other schools in one's own district.

Legislators

Building partnerships with legislators can be critical for a school to access much-needed funding and services. When local legislators understand a school's unique demographic and learning needs, they can enact policies and laws that will protect the individual interests of their constituents. How a school positions itself politically in the community can be critical to its success in implementing changes in policies and procedures. Informed legislators can provide testimony in support of a school attempting to implement new and different strategies and policies.

Government Agencies and Nonprofit Organizations

Forging healthy relationships with local, county, state, and national government agencies provides schools with the essential ingredients for enacting policy and leveraging resources effectively and efficiently. When there are questions about how to access governmental resources, a school's healthy relationship with various governmental agencies is critical for its survival. Many student needs—from health care to recreational activities and greater access to family programs—can be met through collaboration with other government agencies and nonprofit organizations.

Outside Funding Organizations

Often, a school finds that it needs financial support beyond that provided through the state and school district to design and implement a program. Outside funding opportunities are often available from nonprofit private and corporate foundations, other governmental agencies, local businesses, community donors, and parents. School sites should create partnerships that encourage the effective use of resources. All resources donated by community partners can be advertised in the school's communication publications. Fundraising activities include securing financial donations; participating in volunteer programs; donating products, gifts-in-kind, and services; sponsoring events; donating capital equipment and services; donating facilities; and collaborating with other groups to leverage resources.

Identifying the Roles of Various Stakeholder Groups

The first step in taking advantage of all that these stakeholders have to offer is to identify them and ascertain what each can do to help support the daily operations of your school. Figure 2.1 provides a sample form for identifying stakeholders and their roles in your school.

FIGURE 2.1. Identification of Stakeholders and Their Roles in Your School

Stakeholder group: _____

Roles: _____

Stakeholder group: _____

Roles: _____

Stakeholder group: _____

Roles: _____

Stakeholder group: _____

Roles: _____

Stakeholder group: _____

Roles: _____

Stakeholder group: _____

Roles: _____

Stakeholder group: _____

Roles: _____

Policies and Procedures That Support School and Community Partnerships

3

▪ ▪

In this chapter, we describe in detail the policies and procedures that support school and community partnerships, including program monitoring, school safety, volunteer supervision, and support of the volunteers at the school. We also discuss the importance of continued recruitment activities to ensure enough volunteers to implement your program goals. These policies are essential to the successful implementation of a strong volunteer cohort at a school—an essential component of any community-empowered school.

The School's Structure to Support Partnerships

Research suggests that successful site-managed schools rely on decision-making representation from all stakeholder groups to ensure healthy partnership development (Henderson, Marburger, & Ooms, 1986). Schools that support community involvement must include representation of all stakeholder groups in program delivery and policymaking decisions. When the concerns of various stakeholder groups are considered in the decision-making process, there will be increased acceptance of new programs from the greater school community.

For example, supplementary social services are frequently offered to a school's students and their families through a site-based parent center. Many of these centers are able to establish nonprofit tax-exempt status that makes them more effective in raising funds to support their activities. Charter schools, which are generally more independent than site-managed schools, often have enough fiscal autonomy to allow them greater flexibility in building partnerships with community stakeholders through independent access to diverse community resources.

The involvement of all stakeholders places additional responsibilities on the management of a school. It is important to establish a set of policies and procedures that will enable community access to the school site while simultaneously maintaining the school's responsibility for the safety and well-being of the children at the school. These policies must be clearly communicated to the school community on a regular basis.

The following sections present examples of the types of policies and procedures that a school should consider implementing as part of its effort to ensure effective—and safe—use of parent and community volunteers in the classroom, the school, and the greater community. If properly implemented, these procedures will help school volunteers benefit the school and its students.

Monitoring, Supervision, and Volunteer Support Policies

Effective monitoring and support allows volunteers to feel confident in their roles and provides clarity in the structure and design of the volunteer program (Henderson et al., 1986). All schoolwide parent and community volunteer participation programs should include the following components:

- Policies and procedures for the recruitment, processing, use, training, and development of all volunteers for various school support roles

- Schoolwide relationship skill-building training and support for all stakeholders

- Documentation and tracking of all volunteer application forms and health, criminal, and safety checks for each volunteer

- Policies and procedures to support clearly articulated expectations for volunteers

- Grade-level training for classroom volunteers by teachers

- A strategic plan for community problem solving

- Policies and procedures to support community partnership resource development

- Parent and community partnership volunteer career development and recognition

School Safety Policies

To ensure a quality program, all parents and community members who plan to volunteer at the school should complete a volunteer application form. In addition, there are likely to be many state and district-specific requirements that must be met by individuals who will work with children in your school. For example, school volunteers may be required to submit a report from a registered nurse or doctor indicating that they have had a recent tuberculosis (TB) skin test or chest X-ray that indicates no sign of TB. Establishment of policies to ensure that every volunteer receives the appropriate TB skin test and has it checked by a qualified individual, and to make sure that the school has a record of when every volunteer needs an updated test, are essential to the smooth operation of this important concern.

In other locations, it may be necessary to fingerprint volunteers and submit the fingerprints to a criminal check and review. Volunteers should not be permitted to work at the school until this procedure is complete.

Once the volunteer's fingerprint card is cleared by an appropriate government agency and the TB skin test is cleared by a registered nurse, the volunteer's application form can be processed by the school. At this point, the school should invite the volunteer to attend an orientation that provides more information about the types of volunteer activities available at the school. If possible, each volunteer should have his or her picture taken for a volunteer identification badge. A badge provides a basic level of security, indicating the individual is cleared to be on campus, and also offers volunteers a visible token of belonging to the school community. It is the responsibility of the school administration to maintain volunteer documents and ensure that all volunteers meet necessary state, local, and school requirements.

Some schools also provide liability insurance for school volunteers. This insurance typically protects volunteers working at the school on school business. Some schools create policies that state that volunteers should not drive students other than their own children back and forth to school to minimize liability to volunteers. School policies should also state that parents and community volunteers not provide school services off site beyond the traditional school program. If a volunteer has had a previous relationship with a student in the school, that relationship exists completely outside of the school program and the school should not assume any responsibility regarding it. Policies should be developed for volunteers regarding emergency evacuation procedures, child abuse reporting, sexual harassment procedures, appropriate classroom behavior and dress codes, baby-sitting and classroom attendance of younger siblings, and confidentiality procedures when working with students.

Volunteer Recruitment Policies and Procedures

The continued recruitment of school volunteers is a never-ending task. It is recommended that the school establish the position of a school and community partnership coordinator who will organize all volunteer, teacher, and staff recruitment activities and training and supervise all schoolwide volunteer activities. The school should establish a calendar of recruitment and training activities to support the mission of the school and the function of the volunteer program in its support of the school's mission. Typically, most effective volunteer recruitment programs are designed to coincide with the beginning of the school year. Although there are always things that need to be done in a school, and the need for volunteers may appear greater than the supply, it is important that the school have activities identified and ready for volunteers to do. There is nothing worse than having many volunteers available at the school with nothing to do.

Volunteer development activities include developing a comprehensive communitywide volunteer recruitment program, providing ongoing training support for the school's teachers and staff, providing ongoing training for the pool of volunteers, providing more intensive grade-level training of volunteers by teachers, and providing ongoing volunteer career development and recognition. The school and community partnership coordinator should oversee all organizational and training activities. The coordinator is also responsible for identifying new opportunities for the use of volunteers at the school site.

Training

An important component of any successful volunteer effort is training. Training is essential for both the volunteers from the community and teachers and other school staff. Understanding each other's role at the school and how each group can best be used will improve the operation of the school and make the volunteer program a success.

Ongoing Professional Development for Teachers

Once the school initiates an aggressive volunteer recruitment program, it should hold an initial staff development session in which teachers and staff have an opportunity to create specific grade-level plans for the use of their volunteers. This will form the outline for the training session. In addition, training should acquaint teachers and volunteers with effective tutoring and mentoring models and classroom strategies for various grade levels. The training session should also describe the school's volunteer recruitment and training program and indicate how teachers can both support volunteer recruitment and use the volunteers.

In Chapter 4, we provide examples of staff development agendas, grade-level volunteer use plans, sample volunteer program policies and procedures, and sample training handouts that have been successful in the past.

Parent and Community Volunteer
Training Plan for Grade-Level Support

After the teachers complete their training and grade-level plans, they can actively recruit grade-level parents and community volunteers at back-to-school nights and events. The school can provide each teacher with its volunteer application packet for completion. Once parents and volunteers complete the school application process and attend a schoolwide informational meeting on how to support teachers in the classroom, classroom teachers or clusters of grade-level teachers can further train volunteers. These grade-level trainings can teach parents and community volunteers how to successfully tutor and mentor students using the grade-level curriculum materials.

Parent and Community Partnership Volunteer Career Development and Cross-Training for Additional School Volunteer Opportunities

Once parent and community volunteers become part of a schoolwide volunteer program, the school should help them develop their skills through ongoing career development training and recognition activities. A community-empowered school should create a yearly volunteer development calendar of training and recognition events. In addition to training volunteers on how to effectively support students in the classroom and at the school, professional development workshops can be held for parents and community volunteers on a wide range of topics, including developing effective communication and listening skills, leadership and team building, job development skill building, and career assessment.

Parent and community volunteers can also be provided with weekly schoolwide support meetings at predetermined times in which they can brainstorm solutions for classroom curriculum integration and interactive communications. Volunteers can also share common experiences, brainstorm problem solutions, participate in guest speaker presentations, and receive recognition for outstanding work (Burke & Liljenstolpe, 1992). Volunteer recognition programs can include ceremonial presentations at planned meals with student entertainment, student-generated certificates of appreciation, and donated gifts.

Developing a Community Partnership Strategic Plan

Teachers and school administrators can organize community or grade-level family literacy education and community problem-solving meetings. The goals of effective family literacy and community problem-solving meetings include developing district advisory boards for increasing student achievement and family literacy, working with health care and social services agencies in partnering with schools, creating community watches and school safety programs, and expanding community library services and employment development opportunities. Community-empowered schools must draft strategic plans for engaging parents and community volunteers to meet their school's community problem-solving needs at the beginning of each school year. These strategic plans can be managed by school community advisory committees and include representation from all school and community stakeholder groups.

Community Partnership Resource Development Policies and Procedures

School community advisory committees can also develop policies and procedures for securing community partnership resources. The policies and procedures should consider strategic plans for grant development, special events, community donor development, and solicitation of other types of donations.

The creative use of community members, facilities, product donations, and supplies should also be considered as a community resource and as a cost-effective solution to school finance (Burke & Liljenstolpe, 1993). A community-empowered school's enactment of policies and procedures that support school resource use can have a favorable impact on its community's economy (Burke, 1999).

This chapter was devoted to descriptions of the policies, procedures, and training needs of a strong parent and community volunteer program. Chapter 4 provides a detailed set of sample training materials that can be used at any school to establish and successfully operate a strong community-empowered volunteer program.

How to Empower and Train Staff for Effective School and Community Partnerships

Classroom teachers have the ability to help strengthen relationships with students' families and their communities. A student's home environment and cultural life in his or her community are important factors in classroom learning and academic success (McCaleb, 1994). How a teacher incorporates a student's family and community members to support classroom activities is vital for a successful classroom volunteer program. Teachers continue to express apprehension and anxiety regarding how to implement such a program. This chapter provides a detailed training agenda with supporting overheads and worksheets to assist school administrators in training teachers to develop classroom and schoolwide parent and community volunteer programs. The training agenda is divided into 10 components as follows:

1. Overview of effective parent and community volunteer programs

2. Cultural relevancy in using parents, community volunteers, and the community's resources

3. Effective strategies for recruiting parents and community volunteers for the classroom

4. Effective strategies for using and dealing with difficult parents and community volunteers

5. Enriching grade-level curriculum and assessments using parents and community volunteers in the classroom

6. How to design an effective recruitment and use plan using parents and community volunteers

7. Overview of the schoolwide volunteer program

8. Peer mentoring opportunities

9. Sharing a volunteer's cultural experiences

10. Volunteer career development and cross-training

In the pages that follow, we provide detailed materials that, with some modification for the specifics of your school, can be used to train administrators, teachers, and school staff as well as parents and community volunteers to successfully participate in a strong community-empowered school.

As suggested in Chapter 3, the first component of an effective parent and community volunteer program is to provide training for teachers on recruiting and using parent and community volunteers. In the following sections, we describe a 1-day workshop to introduce this topic to teachers.

Workshop Description

In response to the critical need for academic support in public schools, the workshop will examine the basic concepts and skills required for successfully recruiting and training parents and community volunteers to become effective tutors and mentors for diverse student populations in the classroom. Classroom teachers can bring their parent and volunteer recruitment and use plans for small group evaluation and technical assistance. Ongoing volunteer development support will be available throughout the school year by trained administrators and lead teachers.

Course Objectives

- To acquaint teachers and school staff with various volunteer models and materials

- To expose teachers and staff to specific recruiting and volunteer use strategies for culturally relevant classroom programs

- To demonstrate effective strategies for volunteer and parent assistance in the classroom, tutoring support strategies, cooperative learning strategies for volunteers, and effective volunteer management and training strategies

- To provide practice in parent and volunteer recruitment and classroom use

- To understand the schoolwide volunteer program, including policies, procedures, and training content

- To acquaint teachers and staff with specific strategies for promoting their program to parents and community mentors

Sample Materials

In Figures 4.1 through 4.52, we provide samples of overheads and other materials that can be used in developing the teacher training session described previously. Figures 4.27 through 4.45 are samples of all policies, procedures, grade-level training schedules, and handouts.

FIGURE 4.1. Sample Schedule for Workshop on How to Use Parent and Community Volunteers

9:00–9:30	Part 1: An overview of effective parent and community volunteer programs
9:30–10:00	Part 2: Cultural relevancy in using parents, community volunteers, and community resources in the classroom
10:00–10:30	Part 3: Effective strategies for recruiting parent and community volunteers for the classroom
10:30–10:45	Break
10:45–11:15	Part 4: Effective strategies for using and dealing with difficult parent and community volunteers in the classroom
11:15–11:45	Part 5: Enriching grade-level curriculum and assessments using parent and community volunteers in the classroom
11:45–12:10	Part 6: How to design an effective volunteer recruitment and use plan using parent and community volunteers in the classroom
12:10–1:00	Working lunch on designing a grade-level recruitment and use plan
1:00–2:00	Sample recruitment and use plans for each grade level
2:00–3:00	Part 7: Overview of the schoolwide volunteer program with policies, procedures, schoolwide informational meeting, and volunteer training
3:00–3:15	Part 8: Peer mentoring opportunities using parent and community volunteers in the classroom
3:15–3:45	Part 9: Sharing a volunteer's cultural experiences for program planning
3:45–4:15	Part 10: Volunteer career development and cross-training for additional school volunteer training opportunities

FIGURE 4.2. Pretraining Evaluation on How to Use Parent and Community Volunteers in the Classroom

Consider the following statements as they relate to your usage of volunteers in the classroom and circle the appropriate numerical value (1 for high and 5 for low) for each:

	High				**Low**
1. Parent participation for students is important.	1	2	3	4	5
2. Classroom participation for parents contributes to students' academic success.	1	2	3	4	5
3. Recruiting community volunteers to support students' academic achievement is important.	1	2	3	4	5
4. It is important to include community volunteers at the school to increase the community's understanding about the school.	1	2	3	4	5
5. I can work with up to four volunteers a day to support students' literacy skills.	1	2	3	4	5
6. I am not confident working with classroom volunteers.	1	2	3	4	5
7. Most community tutoring programs are fragmented.	1	2	3	4	5
8. Illiterate parent and community volunteers provide limited academic support services.	1	2	3	4	5
9. I can identify at least four parent or community volunteers who would be helpful as classroom tutors or mentors.	1	2	3	4	5
10. I am confident recruiting parent and community volunteers.	1	2	3	4	5
11. I am confident about how to use volunteers in my classroom.	1	2	3	4	5
12. Managing and training volunteers is challenging.	1	2	3	4	5

FIGURE 4.3. Part 1 Overhead for Workshop Group Activity

Identify Teacher Experience and Knowledge

List effective parent and community mentorship and tutoring programs
in schools that you have observed or researched:

1.

2.

3.

4.

5.

6.

7.

8.

9.

10.

11.

12.

FIGURE 4.4. Part 1 Overhead for Workshop Training

An Overview of Effective Parent and Community Volunteer Programs

❏ Mentoring relationship types include providing students with companionship, academic tutoring, career and professional guidance, and basic life skills reinforcement.

❏ Epstein's framework of parent involvement describes the six types of activities (Epstein, Coates, Salinas, Sanders, & Simon, 1997):

  • Type 1: Parenting support activities include helping families establish home environments that support their children's academic achievement.

  • Type 2: Communicating activities include creating effective communications between the school and the home.

  • Type 3: Volunteering support includes the recruitment and organization of a comprehensive school and classroom parent and community volunteer program.

  • Type 4: Learning at-home strategies include providing families with information about how to help students with their homework and school activities.

  • Type 5: Decision-making practices include parents in the school's decision-making process.

  • Type 6: Community collaboration activities include organizing and using community-based services to support the school's programs.

❏ Parent and community volunteer education programs can include family literacy projects, parent education, classroom support and academic content training, home visits, assisting with curriculum development, and academic enrichment activities.

❏ Schools can eliminate obstacles to creating effective parent and community partnerships by instituting the following practices (Far West Laboratory, 1992):

  • Schools can offer weekend and evening meetings to assist parents and community members in overcoming feelings of discomfort, transportation problems, and lack of child care.

  • Translation services can be provided at meetings for second-language learners.

  • Schools can provide school notices, home visits, and telephone calls in the home language.

  • When recruiting parents and community members, the emphasis should be kept on supporting students' academic success.

  • Schools should reward adult volunteers and celebrate progress.

❏ For home visits, essential communication skills include empathic listening, affirmation of the family's strengths, maintaining appropriate boundaries, and modeling effective parenting strategies (Klass, Pettinelli, & Wilson, 1993).

❏ The strategies for parent and community involvement must include the different family members and friends in a child's life. Schools must be sensitive to diverse family configurations and work as a team with all the adults in a child's life (Olsen et al., 1994).

FIGURE 4.5. Part 2 Overhead for Workshop Group Activity

Identifying Strategies for Cultural Relevancy in Using Parents, Community Volunteers, and the Community's Resources in the Classroom

List strategies you have successfully used with your culturally diverse students' families and community members to help them support their students' academic achievement:

1.

2.

3.

4.

5.

6.

7.

8.

9.

10.

11.

12.

FIGURE 4.6. Part 2 Overhead for Workshop Training

Cultural Relevancy in Using Parents, Community Volunteers, and the Community's Resources in the Classroom

❑ Communities of learners from diverse cultures can be built through collaborations among teachers, students, families, and the community. Teachers can facilitate a partnership with students' families and the community through the following practices (McCaleb, 1994):

- Letters should be sent home to students' families in the home language.

- Parents can be encouraged to assist their children's success at school through back-to-school night presentations on the curriculum and by modeling the teacher's teaching methods through classroom participation.

- Teachers must reinforce and value the cultural and linguistic knowledge that students bring from their homes and their community.

- Teachers must become active in the community in which they teach to understand the context of the community.

- Teachers must help students understand the value of what they are learning and encourage collaborative problem solving.

- Students should be encouraged to take responsibility in their community outside of the school.

❑ Cultural relevancy is critical to consider when selecting the actual location for a meeting, when considering how the meeting will be carried out, and when developing creative approaches to promote family literacy (Ada, 1988).

❑ Cultural newcomers need information on the school community and how to enroll their children in their neighborhood school. Once their children are enrolled, newcomers can benefit from parent support groups. Newcomers should be encouraged to participate in school activities with clearly defined roles and responsibilities (Violand-Sanchez, Sutton, & Ware, 1991).

❑ The levels of parent involvement at the school can be influenced by the following factors (Violand-Sanchez et al., 1991):

- The family's length of residence in the United States

- The family's literacy abilities in English and in their native language

- The school's availability of support groups and credentialed bilingual staff

- The family's previous experiences with parent involvement at the school

FIGURE 4.7. Part 3 Overhead for Workshop Group Activity

Effective Strategies for Recruiting Parent and Community Volunteers for the Classroom

List strategies that you have used or observed for effectively recruiting and using parents and community volunteers in your classroom:

1.

2.

3.

4.

5.

6.

7.

8.

9.

10.

11.

12.

FIGURE 4.8. Part 3 Overhead for Workshop Training

Effective Strategies for Recruiting Parent and Community Volunteers for the Classroom

A comprehensive volunteer recruitment and training program will benefit your students' academic success. A thoughtful classroom volunteer job description can help parents and community members determine how they will be used in a specific classroom and what skills they need to support their volunteer role. The following strategies will encourage prospective volunteers to become committed service providers:

❑ Invite volunteers to come into the classroom and observe until they feel comfortable.

❑ Provide informational meetings, and create grade-level workshops.

❑ Answer all questions, and make volunteers feel comfortable and valued.

❑ Make all volunteers feel valued and special.

❑ Do not push volunteers if they are not comfortable.

❑ Do not turn any volunteers away.

❑ Network with parents of students in your class.

❑ Network with your friends, neighbors, and seniors.

❑ Network through community organizations.

❑ Create corporate community service projects for your class.

❑ Use volunteer informational and referral services through nonprofit and government community service groups.

❑ Use rehabilitation training programs.

❑ Recruit through job training programs.

❑ Recruit students who desire work experiences in child development and teaching.

❑ Coordinate volunteer utilization through work study and school project contracts.

❑ Develop educational internships to support special projects.

❑ Form collaborative partnerships with community stakeholders.

❑ Recruit students from local high schools and colleges to support classroom projects.

FIGURE 4.9. Part 3 Overhead for Workshop Training

Sample Daily Classroom Volunteer Job Description

Monday:

1. Verify that all students' names are listed on individual homework sheets.

2. Create a list of nightly homework assignments and duplicate for each student.

3. Assemble a homework packet with weekly assignments for each student and file in each student's communication envelope.

4. Add all school announcement notices in each student's communication envelope.

5. Assist the classroom aide with small group activities in reading, language arts, and math.

6. Before the lunch recess, distribute all communication envelopes to the students to take home.

Tuesday, Wednesday, Thursday:

1. Create classroom teaching aids and student project kits as needed.

2. Assist the classroom aide with small group activities in reading, language arts, and math.

3. Help students complete social studies and science group research projects as assigned.

Friday:

1. Sort all communication materials and homework sheets.

2. Correct all homework sheets, and check off assignments next to each student's name in the homework log.

3. Assist the classroom aide with small group activities in reading, language arts, and math.

FIGURE 4.10. Part 3 Overhead for Workshop Training

School Community Project Contracts Using Classroom Parents and Community Volunteers

❑ Parent and community volunteers help students organize a fundraising literacy read-a-thon and book fair.

❑ Parent volunteers support students in making seasonal art projects for a neighborhood senior center.

❑ Parent and community volunteers help students organize a cultural community fair.

❑ Volunteers help students become advocates for building libraries.

❑ Parent and community volunteers help students participate in a community service learning environmental activity.

❑ Volunteers assist students in food distribution and entertainment at a homeless shelter.

FIGURE 4.11. Part 3 Overhead for Workshop Training

Planning Sheet for Creating School Community Project Contracts

Consider the unique services your students and classroom volunteers can provide to various community groups. In the space provided, describe the projects and identify the community groups with which you can partner for providing these services.

Project description: _____

Community agencies and partners: _____

_____

Project description: _____

Community agencies and partners: _____

_____

FIGURE 4.12. Part 3 Overhead for Workshop Training

Multicultural Considerations for Volunteer Recruitment

❏ The educational system and interpretation of stakeholders' roles vary from country to country and from rural to urban settings (Young & Westernoff, 1996).

❏ Cultural norms, values, and practices will vary within cultures. Being culturally knowledgeable and sensitive to these differences is critical.

❏ Conceptualizations of educational caring should challenge the notion that assimilation is a neutral process (Valenzuela, 1999).

❏ Styles of communicating and personality traits vary among cultures.

❏ Teachers must understand the socioeconomic, linguistic, sociocultural, and structural barriers of diverse cultural groups (Valenzuela, 1999).

❏ Academic achievement is a collective process embedded in a supportive network of culturally diverse social networks (Valenzuela, 1999).

❏ Additional roles for teachers include acting as advocates for the family and helping the family get required services to support their child's academic success (Young & Westernoff, 1996).

❏ A culturally diverse volunteer program bridges the gap in services provided by paid staff.

❏ Cultural diversity among volunteers provides a rich reservoir of talent and curriculum-enrichment opportunities.

❏ Cultural diversity empowers a community to view challenges in new ways (Burke & Liljenstolpe, 1992).

❏ Cultural diversity breeds innovative problem solving and a new conceptualized vision for the future.

❏ Community-empowered schools must introduce a culture of authentic caring that incorporates all stakeholders of a school community (Valenzuela, 1999).

FIGURE 4.13. Part 3 Overhead for Workshop Training

Interview Techniques for Volunteer Recruitment

❑ The interview should be conducted professionally with a pleasant voice.

❑ Listen carefully to the interviewee's language skills to determine his or her literacy level and how well he or she communicates (Burke & Liljenstolpe, 1992).

❑ Through questions, identify the prospective volunteer's strengths, weaknesses, and interests.

❑ Listen for enthusiasm and a positive attitude when discussing the needs of students (Burke & Liljenstolpe, 1992).

❑ Determine the prospective volunteer's sincerity, empathy, professionalism, listening ability, and commitment by asking the volunteer how he or she would handle specific situations.

❑ Structured interviews are intended to keep the prospective volunteer relaxed and talking long enough for the interviewer to determine if the volunteer will have suffi-cient skills for supporting teachers in the classroom (Burke & Liljenstolpe, 1992).

❑ When interviewing, ask open-ended questions that require more than a one-word answer, such as task-related questions.

❑ Ideally, ask each volunteer the same questions to determine the most appropriate assignment.

❑ Discuss any volunteer benefits, including stipends, training programs, and educa-tional opportunities, and review the school's calendar and security policies during the interview.

❑ Determine any special needs the volunteers may have, including a flexible work schedule, transportation, child care, or required training.

❑ Complete the background check, any health exams, and a possible fingerprinting clearance process.

❑ Create work cards and plan for follow-up training sessions.

FIGURE 4.14. Part 4 Overhead for Workshop Group Activity

Effective Strategies for Using and Dealing With Difficult Parent and Community Volunteers in the Classroom

Form small groups of four to six individuals. Consider the various examples of how parent and community volunteers can support teachers in the classroom. Designate a recorder for your group's discussion. Brainstorm specific ways you intend to use volunteers in your classroom. The recorder will be asked to report on your effective volunteer use strategies.

1.

2.

3.

4.

5.

6.

7.

8.

9.

10.

FIGURE 4.15. Part 4 Overhead for Workshop Training

Effective Strategies for Using and Dealing With Difficult Parent and Community Volunteers in the Classroom

❑ Identify strategies for compensating for volunteers who do not show up. Effective strategies include the following:

- Create a list of jobs or job packets with materials that can be done anytime in the classroom, and have them available for a parent who can participate on short notice or for a volunteer who substitutes for another.

- Identify supportive roles that volunteers can provide in the classroom to enrich your program, and have job descriptions available to describe these roles.

- Be flexible and adaptable when working with volunteers, and view their roles as a supplementary enrichment component to your program.

❑ Identify strategies for approaching and redirecting distracting volunteers.

- Remind volunteers that they are present to help students achieve.

- Model appropriate student support behavior for volunteers.

- Redirect volunteers when necessary, and emphasize the importance of their behavior for the success of the volunteer program.

- Set clear limits for appropriate classroom behavior with consequences for infractions.

❑ Consider strategies for correcting volunteers who use using inappropriate behavior or tutoring strategies.

- Train volunteers on how to work with students.

- Model appropriate strategies for supporting students.

- Have experienced volunteers mentor new volunteers.

❑ Set clear limits for volunteer troublemakers and know-it-alls.

- Train volunteers in the appropriate behavior that must be used with students, and identify the consequences when appropriate behavior is not consistently used.

- Establish a procedure for redirecting volunteer activities outside of the classroom.

- Establish a procedure for transferring ineffective volunteers to other schoolwide volunteer efforts.

- Remain positive and consistent, and always put the needs of students first.

❏ Intimidated parent and community volunteers need extra encouragement.

- Partner the intimidated volunteer with an experienced volunteer for reinforcement.

- Provide positive feedback when appropriate.

- Keep the assignments simple until the timid volunteer gains self-confidence.

- Allow the intimidated volunteer to initially observe the class, and eventually give him or her increased responsibilities.

❏ Terminate a volunteer relationship when all of your strategies for retraining, modeling, and redirecting fail. Reassign the volunteer to other schoolwide volunteer opportunities.

❏ Develop strategies for involving school administrators to reinforce the quality of your volunteer program.

❏ Create a classroom volunteer calendar highlighting the schoolwide and grade-level training opportunities for volunteers throughout the school year.

❏ Parents are students' first teachers. When properly trained, parents and other significant volunteers can reinforce in the home the concepts taught by teachers.

- Parents and community volunteers must learn from the teacher's modeling and transfer this knowledge to other family members.

- Community volunteers can provide a significant emotional and academic impact on a student's life when parents are not available.

FIGURE 4.16. Part 5 Overhead for Workshop Group Activity

Enriching Grade-Level Curriculum and Assessments Using Parent and Community Volunteers in the Classroom

Brainstorm specific ways you intend to use volunteers to enrich your grade-level curriculum and help you assess your program needs. Consider curriculum-enrichment strategies that can be used at other grade levels.

1.

2.

3.

4.

5.

6.

7.

8.

9.

10.

11.

12.

FIGURE 4.17. Part 5 Overhead for Workshop Training

Enriching Grade-Level Curriculum and Assessments Using Parent and Community Volunteers in the Classroom

❑ The time that parent and community volunteers spend with children in an enjoyable academic activity can have a significant impact on all students. The following is a list of effective strategies for engaging parent and community volunteers to support students' academic achievement:

• Parent and community volunteers can transcribe student stories on large butcher paper or on the computer. Once the stories are written, students can illustrate their stories, read them to an audience of younger students, or create a play using the story as the plot.

• The volunteer can read a story to students, and students can make up their own story ending with illustrations.

• Parent and community volunteers can make family memory books with a student's collected stories.

• A volunteer can read a rhyming story to students and have students create new rhyming words.

❑ Audio books can be used by volunteers and students. These audio books provide a new reader with the opportunity to follow the print and assimilate the pattern of the story.

❑ Parents and volunteers can encourage students to read books that generate high interest but that are more difficult to read.

❑ Children should be encouraged to read aloud to adults from other cultures and with different reading abilities.

❑ Parent and community volunteers can help students create books about their families, with each page of a book featuring one family member.

FIGURE 4.18. Part 6 Overhead for Workshop Group Activity

How to Design an Effective Recruitment and Use Plan Using Parent and Community Volunteers in the Classroom

List four primary goals for your academic program:

1.

2.

3.

4.

Based on these goals, list four support roles that parent and community volunteers can provide in the classroom:

1.

2.

3.

4.

What supplementary and assessment roles can parent and community volunteers provide you?

1.

2.

3.

How can these supplementary services support other classroom activities?

What skills are required to support your various language arts volunteer opportunities?

1.

2.

3.

4.

What specific recruitment strategies do you intend to use to recruit up to four volunteers in your class each day?

1.

2.

3.

4.

What strategies will you use to approach these individuals for your program?

1.

2.

3.

What specific training components will you include for volunteer development?

1.

2.

3.

4.

What resource and training support do you need from your administrative staff to be successful in your recruitment, training, and use efforts?

FIGURE 4.19. Sample Kindergarten Recruitment and Use Plan Using Parent and Community Volunteers in the Classroom

List four primary goals for your academic program:

1. Phonemic awareness

2. Letter recognition

3. Letter formation through handwriting

4. Exposure to enriching literature

Based on these goals, list four support roles that parent and community volunteers can provide in the classroom:

1. Play games to reinforce phonemic awareness

2. Kinesthetic activities to reinforce language arts

3. Record cassettes to build listening skills

4. Listen to individual and small group reading

What supplementary and assessment roles can parent and community volunteers provide you?

1. Make journals and handwriting booklets

2. Take dictation in student journals

3. Provide weekly assessment of phonemic awareness

How can these supplementary services support other classroom activities?

The services will allow teachers to work more with the students during the instructional day.

What skills are required to support your various language arts volunteer opportunities?

1. Effective communication and social skills

2. The ability to follow directions

3. A desire to learn literacy skills

4. Patience

What specific recruitment strategies do you intend to use to recruit up to four volunteers in your class each day?

1. I will invite parents to observe my classroom, and I will enforce an open-door policy.

2. Parent meetings will be held each month.

3. I will ask volunteers to recruit other family members or friends to participate.

4. I will talk to other teachers about having older students assist in the classroom.

What strategies will you use to approach these individuals for your program?

1. I will ask them face-to-face when I see them.

2. I will contact them on the telephone.

3. I will send a letter home with the students.

What specific training components will you include for volunteer development?

1. I will train them on classroom computers.

2. I will model how to individually work with students.

3. I will train them in child development and effective grade-level expectations.

4. I will train them in behavior management.

What resource and training support do you need from your administrative staff to be successful in your recruitment, training, and use efforts?

1. I need more time to train the volunteers.

2. I need bilingual literature handouts on behavior management topics, child development, and grade-level standards.

FIGURE 4.20. Sample First-Grade Recruitment and Use Plan Using Parent and Community Volunteers in the Classroom

List four primary goals for your academic program:

1. Approach reading fluency

2. Read for comprehension

3. Begin to write in an organized structure

4. Motivate students to be life-long readers

Based on these goals, list four support roles that parent and community volunteers can provide in the classroom:

1. Read to students

2. Listen to students read

3. Discuss what was read with students

4. Augment themes by providing supplementary books

What supplementary and assessment roles can parent and community volunteers provide you?

1. Provide one-on-one assistance as necessary

2. Support phonemic assessment

3. Maintain a log of student reading

How can these supplementary services support other classroom activities?

These services provide one-on-one reading and writing assistance in any subject.

What skills are required to support your various language arts volunteer opportunities?

1. A positive attitude

2. Basic computer literacy skills to support computer activities

3. High motivation and effective listening skills

4. Nurturing and support

What specific recruitment strategies do you intend to use to recruit up to four volunteers in your class each day?

1. Recruit at a continental breakfast

2. Provide personal invitations at parent conferences

3. Conduct a phone survey to discuss class interests

4. Distribute thank-you notes to those who volunteer

What strategies will you use to approach these individuals for your program?

1. Make phone calls

2. Provide direct communication with parents

3. Invite parents to school activities

What specific training components will you include for volunteer development?

1. Train volunteers on the phonics program

2. Train volunteers and students on basic sentence structure

3. Teach volunteers and students basic technical writing

4. Model appropriate volunteer behavior in the classroom

What resource and training support do you need from your administrative staff to be successful in your recruitment, training, and use efforts?

1. Train parents on effective time management strategies

2. Help parents and volunteers develop effective communication strategies

3. Train family members on computer literacy skills

FIGURE 4.21. Sample Second-Grade Recruitment and Use Plan Using Parent and Community Volunteers in the Classroom

List four primary goals for your academic program:

1. Develop an appreciation for reading
2. Demonstrate the ability to predict events in a reading passage
3. Develop effective communication and listening skills
4. Increase writing proficiency skills

Based on these goals, list four support roles that parent and community volunteers can provide in the classroom:

1. Assist students in editing their work
2. Lead discussion groups with students
3. Act as a reading buddy with small groups of students
4. Maintain a tape-recording log of students reading various passages

What supplementary and assessment roles can parent and community volunteers provide you?

1. Encourage high-level thinking skills by guiding students' decision making and asking clarification questions
2. Support phonemic and phonetic student assessments
3. Orally assess a student's comprehension and critical-thinking reading abilities
4. Help students create a play, puppet show, art project, or Saturday workshop

How can these supplementary services support other classroom activities?

This provides the teacher with more preparation and planning time.

What skills are required to support your various language arts volunteer opportunities?

1. Patience in working with students
2. Respect for the students and their teachers
3. Effective interpersonal skills
4. Consistent and reliable support

What specific recruitment strategies do you intend to use to recruit up to four volunteers in your class each day?

1. Invite volunteers to attend field trips to learn more about a grade-level program

2. Solicit information about parents' talents from their children

3. Recruit parent and community volunteers at meetings

4. Personal notes and follow-up phone calls

What strategies will you use to approach these individuals for your program?

1. Approach a parent about his or her potential talent and ask the parent for help

2. Remind parents that I need their help to support student achievement

3. Recruit parent volunteers through the parent center

What specific training components will you include for volunteer development?

1. Leadership development training

2. Creativity and initiative skill building

3. Oral, reading, and writing competency development

4. Interpersonal communication skills

What resource and training support do you need from your administrative staff to be successful in your recruitment, training, and use efforts?

1. Support from the program coordinator

2. Coordination and collaboration from peer teachers

3. How to train parents to effectively support teachers in the classroom

4. How to support limited English-proficient volunteers for volunteer development

FIGURE 4.22. Sample Third-Grade Recruitment and Use Plan Using Parent and Community Volunteers in the Classroom

List four primary goals for your academic program:

1. Students will be able to read at or above grade level.

2. Students will develop effective reading comprehension skills.

3. Students will be able to demonstrate increased writing skills, including spelling, grammar, increased vocabulary usage, and effective editing.

4. Students will be able to publish their writing assignments using computer technology.

Based on these goals, list four support roles that parent and community volunteers can provide in the classroom:

1. Volunteers will observe students' book selections for reading.

2. They will facilitate literature discussions.

3. They will assist with computer usage.

4. Volunteers will assist teachers with lesson preparations.

What supplementary and assessment roles can parent and community volunteers provide you?

1. They can record students as they read.

2. They can chart students' answers.

3. They can help students edit their work.

How can these supplementary services support other classroom activities?

These services can support students when using their literary skills for all subject areas.

What skills are required to support your various language arts volunteer opportunities?

1. Effective language arts skills in the primary classroom language

2. Creativity

3. Showing initiative

4. Student management

What specific recruitment strategies do you intend to use to recruit up to four volunteers in your class each day?

1. The college placement office

2. Educational internships

3. Post recruitment at libraries

4. School project contracts

What strategies will you use to approach these individuals for your program?

1. Tell people about the school's need for volunteers

2. Offer parents the opportunity to provide support services at home

3. Use older students as peer tutors

What specific training components will you include for volunteer development?

1. Ensure commitment from volunteers

2. Provide effective study-skill development for classroom support

3. Give an overview of the academic program content

4. Teach volunteers how to manage time and multiple priorities

What resource and training support do you need from your administrative staff to be successful in your recruitment, training, and use efforts?

1. The opportunity to observe other successful grade-level volunteer support programs in the school or district

2. A way to incorporate the help of student peer tutors

3. Ways to organize home projects for parent volunteers who wish to support the teachers outside of the classroom

FIGURE 4.23. Sample Fourth-Grade Recruitment and Use Plan Using Parent and Community Volunteers in the Classroom

List four primary goals for your academic program:

1. Develop English language mastery

2. Develop fluent reading skills

3. Increase reading comprehension to grade level

4. Develop effective communication skills

Based on these goals, list four support functions that parent and community volunteers can provide in the classroom:

1. Remedial reading assistance to individual students

2. Development of writing skills through word processing

3. Supervision of independent writing practice

4. Vocabulary development through flash cards

With what supplementary and assessment activities can parent and community volunteers assist you?

1. Administering reading assessment

2. Correcting language arts homework

3. Assisting with an art project related to language arts development

How can these supplementary services support other classroom activities?

These skills can support students in all curricular areas.

What skills are required to support your various language arts volunteer opportunities?

1. The ability to read

2. Proper grammar

3. Dependability

4. The ability to work independently

From what groups do you intend to recruit up to four volunteers in your class each day?

1. College students in teacher preparation programs

2. Students working on community service projects

3. Retired teachers

4. Family and friends of students and network with service groups

What strategies will you use to approach these individuals for your program?

1. Invite potential volunteers to various activities

2. Hold an end-of-term party to support recruitment and showcase the program

3. Send home notes inviting parents to support specific projects

What specific training components will you include for volunteer development?

1. Discuss proper and appropriate strategies for student support

2. Demonstrate basic sentence structure to support language arts activities

3. Assist volunteers in developing technology skills for student support

4. Assist volunteers in developing basic printing and cursive writing skills

What resource and training support do you need from your administrative staff to be successful in your recruitment, training, and use efforts?

1. Coordination of the processing of volunteers

2. Team effort from all grade-level teachers

3. Pointers on how to teach parents about child development stages of growth and how these relate to grade-level learning strategies and behavior management

4. Time management strategies for organizing volunteers in the classroom and for adjusting the schedule for absent volunteers

FIGURE 4.24. Sample Fifth-Grade Recruitment and Use Plan Using Parent and Community Volunteers in the Classroom

List four primary goals for your academic program:

1. Write concise paragraphs with proper grammar and sentence structure
2. Read and comprehend substantive text passages
3. Develop effective communication skills
4. Apply effective language arts skills to math, science, and social studies

Based on these goals, list four ways that parent and community volunteers can help in the classroom:

1. Provide one-on-one reading assistance
2. Facilitate a readers theater acting out parts of various literature passages and integrate the skills of predicting and drawing new conclusions
3. Help students develop and present written and oral book reports
4. Help students conduct research on the Internet for a report

With what supplementary and assessment activities can parent and community volunteers assist you?

1. Training parents who cannot volunteer in the classroom to help their children at home
2. Managing various research and performing arts projects for teachers
3. Helping with classroom clerical duties

How can these supplementary services support other classroom activities?

These services can also be used to support performing arts activities, science experiments, and multicultural lessons and to organize guest speakers.

What skills are required to support your various language arts volunteer opportunities?

1. English fluency and literacy
2. Outgoing personality and confidence in managing student behavior in group situations
3. Sensitivity to individual learning styles
4. Effective communication skills

What specific recruitment strategies do you intend to use to recruit up to four volunteers in your class each day?

1. Contact chamber of commerce
2. Contact local high schools
3. Recruit at churches
4. Recruit community leaders as guest speakers

What strategies will you use to approach these individuals for your program?

1. I will approach individuals through phone calls.
2. Students, teachers, and volunteers could invite various community leaders to a grade-level event.
3. I will ask contacts to introduce me to other leaders and groups.

What specific training components will you include for volunteer development?

1. Teach volunteers how to work with the teacher assistant and teacher for coordination
2. Have a monthly volunteer support group meeting for problem solving and support
3. Model effective teaching and behavior management strategies for volunteers
4. Provide volunteers with child development and learning strategies handouts

What resource and training support do you need from your administrative staff to be successful in your recruitment, training, and use efforts?

1. I need guidance on how to provide volunteers with feedback about their classroom performance.
2. I need guidance on how to manage a difficult volunteer when redirection does not work.
3. I need staff support regarding how to help volunteers obtain materials to support performing arts activities in the classroom.
4. I need assistance in helping volunteers develop leadership skills beyond the classroom to support the school in its decision-making process.
5. I want to learn how to train volunteers in conducting effective student observations.
6. I need opportunities for volunteers to observe other classrooms in which volunteers are effectively working with students in small groups.

FIGURE 4.25. Part 7 Overhead for Workshop Group Activity

Overview of the Schoolwide Volunteer Program With Policies, Procedures, Schoolwide Informational Meeting, and Grade-Level Volunteer Training

List topics that should be covered in a schoolwide orientation and that a teacher should cover in a grade-level volunteer training:

1.

2.

3.

4.

5.

6.

7.

8.

9.

10.

11.

12.

FIGURE 4.26. Part 7 Overhead for Workshop Training

Overview of the Schoolwide Volunteer Program With Policies, Procedures, Schoolwide Informational Meeting, and Grade-Level Volunteer Training

After teachers have recruited prospective parent and community volunteers for their classrooms, all prospective volunteers should attend a schoolwide volunteer informational meeting that will include discussion of the following topics:

❑ The role of the volunteer in the school

❑ The application process and completion of forms

❑ The volunteer dress code

❑ The volunteer responsibility code and letter of agreement

❑ Volunteer resources for effective listening, reading, and writing support

❑ The grade-level training schedule

❑ Grade-level training meetings and handouts

FIGURE 4.27. Sample Schoolwide Volunteer Program Memo to Teachers

September 10, 200X

To: All Teachers

From: The School and Community Partnership Coordinator

Re: The School's Volunteer Program

Attached you will find a parent letter that briefly explains our goal of enhancing our existing volunteer program. Our new **Volunteers at Home and in Our Community Program** is expanding to include our community at large. Our goal is to add to our existing parent involvement program. At your back-to-school meeting with parents, please distribute the attached volunteer recruitment letter and invite all parents and community members to attend one of the volunteer informational meetings scheduled on September 17 at 7:00 a.m., 3:00 p.m., or 7:00 p.m. At the volunteer informational meeting, we will describe our school's volunteer development program, define the role of a volunteer, review our volunteer policies and procedures, and provide prospective volunteers with follow-up resources and training.

If you have any questions, please do not hesitate to contact me. I am here to provide you with the training and resources required for implementing a successful parent and community volunteer program.

FIGURE 4.28. Sample Schoolwide Volunteer Program Recruitment Letter

September 10, 200X

Dear Family Members and Friends,

   This year we are making a special effort to have our school become a place where your children feel comfortable, cared for, and included. We want our students' family members to feel especially welcome. We are calling this effort our **Volunteers at Home and in Our Community Program.** The idea is to expand our existing schoolwide community activities and develop new activities to respond to the changing needs of our school community's families. We hope this program will help you and your children feel that you are part of a caring school community.

   There will be many additional opportunities for you and your children to become involved at school. You will receive updated information about how you can help us by volunteering with a team of staff, parents, and community members who will create and organize community-building activities throughout the year.

   We would like to invite you to an informational meeting to learn more about the **Volunteers at Home and in Our Community Program.** If you are interested in helping out your school, please join us at one of the following meetings:

Monday, September 17, 200X at the School Parent Center

7:00 a.m.–8 a.m.; 3:00 p.m.–4:00 p.m.; 7:00 p.m.–8:00 p.m.

Child care and refreshments will be provided.

Sincerely,

The School and Community Partnership Coordinator

FIGURE 4.29. Sample Schoolwide Volunteer Program Informational Meeting Agenda

Welcome: Introduce the school's administration and volunteer support staff

Icebreaker: Share a successful volunteer experience and how you felt

Overview of the Volunteer Program and Description of Volunteer Opportunities

The Role of the Volunteer:

The Application Process and Forms

TB Skin Testing Schedule and Fingerprinting Schedule

Dress Code

Volunteer Responsibility Code

Volunteer Agreement

Volunteer Resources for Program Success:

10 Tips for Effective Listening Skills

10 Tips for Reading With Students

10 Tips for Helping Students Write

Additional Schedules for Grade-Level Training Meetings

FIGURE 4.30. Sample Schoolwide Volunteer Program Application Form

Name: _____ Home phone number: _____

Address: _____

List all names and grade levels of your children who attend our school: _____

_____

_____

Your social security number or driver's license number: _____

Employer's name: _____ Work phone number: _____

Do you have any medical condition that we need to be aware of? _____

_____

Date of TB skin test clearance: _____

Date of fingerprinting clearance: _____

Check the following volunteer activities that you would like to support:

Clerical _____ After-school enrichment _____

Yard duty _____ Saturday enrichment _____

Facilities and maintenance _____ At-home curriculum support _____

Classroom support and tutoring _____ Evening parent education _____

Child care and parent center _____ Other _____

List the types of volunteer training and career development training you would like

to receive: _____

_____

Your emergency contact's name: _____

Relationship to you: _____

Emergency contact's phone number: _____

FIGURE 4.31. Sample Schoolwide Volunteer Program Dress Code

All school volunteers are asked to comply with the dress code established as a schoolwide standard for professional attire and safety. Please read the list carefully and sign to indicate that you agree to comply with this code.

1. Midriffs must be covered.

2. Shorts, skirts, and dresses must be no shorter than mid-thigh length.

3. Clothes can be tailored but not so tight as to fit like a second skin.

4. Clothing should not look provocative or sexy.

5. Tops should not be low cut or revealing.

6. Pants may be loose but not baggy like gang attire.

7. Men must wear shirts with sleeves.

8. Undergarments must not be visible.

9. Shoes must be closed toe and have some support around the heel.

I agree to comply with this dress code.

Name: _____

Signature: _____

Date: _____

FIGURE 4.32. Sample Schoolwide Volunteer Program Responsibility Code

To protect the health and safety of students, proper volunteer behavior at school is an essential element of the total school program. Our school site plan expands this code and states that the entire school community (students, teachers, staff, administrators, parents, and community members) will work cooperatively and collaboratively together to create a child-centered environment in which all stakeholders are empowered by their own sense of ownership and responsibility to the school.

Our school is committed to the goal of providing each student with every opportunity to develop his or her capabilities to the fullest extent possible. The teacher acts legally in place of the parent while his or her child is in school. The teacher is the dominant figure in the implementation of the intended curriculum.

Please read the following statement and sign where indicated:

I agree to support and cooperate with the school's Volunteer Responsibility Code as indicated by my signature.

Volunteer's Signature _____ **Date** _____

FIGURE 4.33. Sample Schoolwide Volunteer Program Agreement

As a participating volunteer of this school, I agree to abide by the following volunteer policies and procedures: Please check all program components and sign and date at the bottom of the page:

AGREED COMMITMENTS

_____ I agree to attend the volunteer informational meeting.

_____ I agree to complete the application forms, the TB skin test, and the fingerprint clearance process.

_____ I agree to submit all completed forms to the School and Community Partnership Coordinator.

_____ I agree to attend the grade-level volunteer training.

_____ I agree to abide by the school dress code and volunteer policies.

_____ I agree to be on time for scheduled meetings and contact the coordinator if I plan to miss a scheduled session.

_____ I agree to keep discussions about individual students confidential.

_____ I agree to accept training from the coordinator, staff, and teachers.

_____ I agree to abide by all school rules at all times and to consider the needs of the students first.

_____   _____

Signature   **Date**

FIGURE 4.34. Sample Schoolwide Volunteer Program Orientation Training Handout

10 Tips for Effective Listening Skills

1. Listen for contextual understanding.

2. Respectfully accept the speaker's perspective.

3. Eliminate assumptions.

4. Ask clarifying questions to increase comprehension.

5. Ask sequencing questions for added clarification.

6. Listen for facts, feelings, and the main ideas.

7. Paraphrase for understanding.

8. Create a supportive environment for listening.

9. Eliminate distractions.

10. Identify obstacles to clearly hearing what is being said.

FIGURE 4.35. Sample Schoolwide Volunteer Program Orientation Training Handout

10 Tips for Reading With Students

1. Select books and book passages that students can relate to and find entertaining (Perkins, 1995).

2. Practice reading the story aloud before you read it to the students.

3. Vary your expression, tone, pace, and volume for emphasis. Read a fast-moving action scene quickly and a suspenseful part slowly.

4. Set the stage and time period, and use illustrations to emphasize key concepts. Before beginning the story, ask the students questions to help set the stage. If the students need background information to appreciate the context of the story, spend time explaining key concepts.

5. Have students predict the story from the title, the pictures, or the first paragraph. Stop occasionally while reading the story, and ask the students to predict what will happen next.

6. Many students have difficulty listening to a story for any sustained period of time. If the students are distracted, stop reading the story and have the students draw what is going on in the story or retell the story to you to increase their comprehension.

7. If you are reading a picture book, review the details in the pictures and how they relate to the story. Are there any clues to the story's content in the pictures?

8. Talk about the story after you have finished reading. Questions may include:
   - How do you feel about _____?
   - What do you think happens after the book is ended?
   - If you could write a follow-up to the story, what would you put in it?
   - Why do you think this story could or could not happen?
   - What parts of the story don't you believe?
   - Would you like to have a character in the story for a friend?
   - Why do you think this author wrote this book?
   - Could any of the events in the story have happened in the author's life?
   - Would you like to read another story by this author?

9. Discuss new vocabulary words, and identify appropriate definitions.

10. Discuss how the story was constructed, and study sentence structure, the story's setting, and each character's development.

FIGURE 4.36. Sample Schoolwide Volunteer Program Orientation Training Handout

10 Tips for Helping Students Write

To encourage students, do not become preoccupied by the students' spelling and grammar usage. Students can support each other's writing improvement by editing each other's work when they are completing significant projects for publication, distribution, or display. The following ideas can expand writing opportunities for students:

1. Encourage students to write cards and notes to friends and family members.

2. Read part or tell part of a story, and have students finish the story. Encourage students to summarize their feelings and ideas about a story or poem.

3. Encourage students to make a picture and write about the drawing.

4. Have students write a heading or title for photographs or pictures.

5. Have students use a journal for writing about their daily feelings. Students and their families can also journalize their family history (Perkins, 1995).

6. Have students write letters to a newspaper editor about a community concern.

7. Have students enter writing contests.

8. Develop a pen pal program with students from another country.

9. Identify a legislative bill that will have an impact on the students' lives, and have them write their opinion to a local legislator.

10. Organize a letter-writing campaign to a school board member in support of a school policy.

FIGURE 4.37. Sample Grade-Level Volunteer Training Letter

Inviting Parents and Community Members

September 19, 200X

Dear Parents and Community Volunteers,

You are invited to a kindergarten training in which we will develop our grade-level plan for the effective use of classroom volunteers and develop skills to support our children's academic success. Our training goals include:

- Identifying strategies for helping our students succeed in school

- Assisting parent and community volunteers to become effective communicators with the students

- Helping parent and community volunteers develop successful strategies for assisting students with their academic programs

Please attend our grade-level training meeting on Monday, September 23, from 7:00 a.m. until 8 a.m. in Room 2. A light breakfast will be served, and child care will be provided.

Sincerely,

Your kindergarten teachers

FIGURE 4.38. Sample Grade-Level Volunteer Training Agenda

7:00-7:15   Refreshments and networking

7:15-7:30   Welcome and breakout presentations in either English or Spanish

- Review the requirements for the volunteer application process, including completing TB skin tests, completing fingerprinting clearance cards, and having pictures taken for the volunteer identification badges.

- Review grade-level safety guidelines, including no food or drink in the classroom, the importance of teacher supervision, the bathroom usage policy for volunteers, and that no younger siblings can be brought into the classroom.

- Discuss age-appropriate behavior management strategies and how parents should limit time spent with their own child. Parents should not help their own child with school projects while volunteering. Volunteers should use questions to help a child solve a problem instead of providing the correct answers.

7:30-7:50   Overview presentations on various classroom support activities, including academic, enrichment, clerical, and work-at-home support activities

7:50-8:00   Parent sign ups for volunteer service on a weekly scheduled basis

FIGURE 4.39. Sample Grade-Level Volunteer Training Letter Requesting a Scheduling Commitment for Classroom Support

September 25, 200X

Dear Parents and Community Volunteers,

This year, I hope to have more parents and community members support my students daily in the classroom. As a classroom volunteer, you will have the opportunity to observe my teaching strategies and at the same time support your child and other students. Please indicate below the days and hours you would be able to help as a volunteer in the classroom.

Name of your student:_____

Name of volunteer: _____ Phone number:_____

_____ **Yes, I/we would like to volunteer in the classroom during the hours below:**

Monday:	8:30-9:50 _____	10:30-11:50 _____
Tuesday:	8:30-9:50 _____	10:30-11:50 _____
Wednesday:	8:30-9:50 _____	10:30-11:50 _____
Thursday:	8:30-9:50 _____	10:30-11:50 _____
Friday:	8:30-9:50 _____	10:30-11:50 _____

_____ **No, I am not able to volunteer in the classroom, but I am able to help with project activities at home.**

Thank you for your support.

Sincerely,

Your Teacher

FIGURE 4.40. Sample Grade-Level Parent Volunteer Training Letter Explaining the Program and Requesting a Scheduling Commitment for Classroom Support

Dear Parents,

A good learning experience is built on a cooperative effort between the parent, child, and teacher. My expectations for conduct and standards for academic growth are high. With your participation in and out of the classroom, we can look forward to a productive, creative, and enjoyable year together.

Children need to have effective role models and warm, loving adults to work with them. If you have a little extra time and the desire, your help would be greatly appreciated. In the past, I have had many parents volunteer their time in the classroom. I encourage this because it provides an opportunity for more children to receive one-on-one attention.

If you are interested in volunteering, please let me know. This can be done on a weekly, biweekly, or occasional basis. The more specialized help students receive in class, the more they learn. I can use volunteers every day of the week. **In the chart below, please list the times you are available for volunteering beside each day of the week.** We will notify you of any requirements for working in the classroom and when we will need you to start.

Day of Week	Times Available
Monday	
Tuesday	
Wednesday	
Thursday	
Friday	
Weekend days	
Various evenings	

Please let me know if you have any specialties or areas of interest that you would like to share with the children. Examples include reading with students, checking students' work, art, math, and working with computers. I am excited about this upcoming school year. I hope we can work together to make the program more significant for all of our students.

Volunteer's Name_____   Student's Name _____

Thank you,

Your Teacher

FIGURE 4.41. Sample Pre- and Post-Grade-Level Volunteer Training Self-Assessment

Consider the following statements as they relate to your usage of volunteers in the classroom, and circle the appropriate numerical value for each:

	High			**Low**	
1. Each family member has specific responsibilities.	1	2	3	4	5
2. Our family has a schedule for sleeping, eating, and completing homework.	1	2	3	4	5
3. We have books in our home that children can read.	1	2	3	4	5
4. I read to my children every evening, or we practice in sustained reading sessions.	1	2	3	4	5
5. My child is encouraged to write letters and to make shopping lists.	1	2	3	4	5
6. My child and I practice math when cooking and while doing household projects.	1	2	3	4	5
7. We discuss our family history and celebrate family rituals and holidays.	1	2	3	4	5
8. I encourage my child to collect, observe, and explore artifacts from nature and science.	1	2	3	4	5
9. Our family talks about daily events and plans for the future.	1	2	3	4	5
10. I encourage my children to enjoy learning and to plan for college.	1	2	3	4	5
11. I am aware of the school policies and procedures, and I know who to contact when there is a problem at the school.	1	2	3	4	5
12. I expect my child to excel in school, and I encourage my child to come to me for support and guidance.	1	2	3	4	5

FIGURE 4.42. Sample 6-Week Grade-Level Training for Parent and Community Volunteers on How to Become an Effective Classroom Volunteer

Workshop Description

In response to the critical need for classroom volunteers to support diverse student populations, the workshop sessions will examine the basic skills required to successfully support teachers. Parent and community volunteers can bring their classroom assistance and child development concerns to small group training sessions for evaluation and technical assistance. Parent and community volunteers will also be trained on how to effectively support the academic needs of culturally and linguistically diverse students. Ongoing training and support will be available through the school's volunteer development program during the school year.

Course Objectives

- To acquaint parent and community volunteers with effective communication and classroom assistance skills

- To expose parent and community volunteers to specific communication strategies for culturally relevant classroom programs

- To demonstrate effective strategies for assisting teachers and students in the classroom, tutoring support strategies, cooperative learning strategies, and how to effectively help students with their academic needs

- To provide practice in effective communication, child development education, and classroom support skills

Weekly Evening Workshop Schedule

7:00–7:30	Icebreaker and weekly updates
7:30–7:50	Activity to develop students' self-esteem
7:50–8:10	Child development topic and group activity
8:10–8:20	Dessert break
8:20–8:40	How to support students' academic achievement
8:40–8:55	How to integrate these volunteer support skills in the classroom activity
8:55–9:00	Homework and wrap-up

(continued)

FIGURE 4.42. Continued

Weekly Themes and Activities

Week #1

Icebreaker: What you want to learn at the workshop brainstorming activity

Self-Esteem: Share something positive that happened to you in the last week with a partner, and actively listen to each other

Child Development Topic: The value of self-esteem

Study Skill Topic: Encouraging sustained reading activities in the home

Classroom Support Strategy: Role-playing clarification questions for reading comprehension

Homework: Self-esteem follow-up; encourage 5 minutes of sustained reading each day, and use clarification questions to reinforce reading comprehension

Week #2

Icebreaker: Homework follow-up

Self-Esteem: Decorate your own unique potato and describe its attributes to a partner

Child Development Topic: Understanding authoritative, permissive, and democratic parent management styles

Study Skill Topic: Effective strategies to support children's homework completion

Classroom Support Strategy: Tutorial support strategies to support academic development and how to use student observation forms

Homework: Self-esteem follow-up activity and helping students with homework

Week #3

Icebreaker: Homework follow-up

Self-Esteem: Evaluate student essays, and write positive comments about each student's essay using Post-it notes

Child Development Topic: Understanding a child's motivation for various types of behavior

Study Skill Topic: How to use math puzzles for problem solving

Classroom Support Strategy: Effective strategies to support students' math development

Homework: Design math puzzles with students

Week #4

Icebreaker: Homework follow-up

Self-Esteem: Observe different parent and child role plays, and practice active listening strategies to increase self-esteem

Child Development Topic: Effective strategies for communicating expectations to develop responsible behavior

Study Skill Topic: How to help students develop journal writing skills and observational strategies for science experimentation

Classroom Support Strategy: Understanding the science experiment process, including collection of materials and data, hypothesis, procedure, and conclusion

Homework: Create a science experiment to develop student observational skills

Week #5

Icebreaker: Homework follow-up

Self-Esteem: Cut out pictures of situations and objects that represent things you like, and share a story about yourself using the pictures as visual aids

Child Development Topic: Understanding natural and logical consequences and determining effective problem-solving strategies for responsible behavior

Study Skill Topic: How to assist students in developing language arts skills through journal writing, letter writing, and making organizational lists

Classroom Support Strategy: How to help students develop their oral and written language skills

Homework: Write a story about a family event with your child

Week #6

Icebreaker: Homework follow-up

Self-Esteem: Create a family coat-of-arms, and discuss the significance of the symbols you designed for your coat-of-arms

Child Development Topic: Family meetings and developing quality time

Study Skill Topic: How to integrate your family's cultural experiences into basic subject skill development

Classroom Support Strategy: How to link students' cultural experiences in social studies units of study

Homework: Create a family history journal with your child

FIGURE 4.43. Sample Letter to Parents on Grade-Level Parent Workshops

September 2, 200X

Dear Parents,

I will be conducting workshops for my first-grade parent volunteers. These workshops are optional and not mandatory. They will be held on Friday mornings from 7:00 a.m. until 7:50 a.m. These workshops will help parents assist me more effectively in the classroom. They will also help parents assist their children with their homework at home. The subjects I will cover include language arts, mathematics, science, and social studies. If there is a large demand for a certain workshop, and volunteer parents cannot attend, I will be happy to reschedule additional workshops on a specific topic at a later date.

The dates for all initial workshops are:

Workshop #	Date	Topic	Content
1	9/10/200X	Language arts	Introduction to the phonic- and literature-based reading programs
2	9/17/200X	Mathematics	Overview of the mathematics curriculum
3	9/24/200X	Social studies	A study of the cultures within the school community
4	10/1/200X	Science	How to observe nature
5	10/8/200X	Make and take	A project will be constructed to use with children to promote family literacy

If you have any questions about any of these workshops, please contact me at extension 225. I look forward to seeing you at the various workshops.

Sincerely,

FIGURE 4.44. Sample Classroom Teacher's Newsletter for Parents

MARCH, 200X

Your Teacher's Monthly Classroom News

Ways You Can Encourage Your Child to Become a Better Reader:

- **Let your child see you read everyday.** What you read doesn't matter. You might read the sports page or a mystery novel. Your child must see you read everyday.

- **Have books and magazines available.** A weekly trip to the library can keep your home filled with good things to read.

- **Limit the time your child spends watching television.**

- **In addition to doing their homework, your child should be expected to do some unassigned reading every day.** Reading gets better with practice.

- **Set aside some time for family reading and talking about reading.** Young children should be read to every day. Children are never too old to enjoy listening to an adult read. It's also really fun to discuss and exchange ideas about your favorite parts in a story, what might happen next, comparisons to other books by the same author, and many other topics.

What's New in Our Classroom:

Volunteers: Since our aide has had a new baby and is not returning, it may take awhile before our class will have a new aide. If you would like to volunteer in the classroom, please let me know a day in advance. I have parents who volunteer in the classroom every week at the same time, which is wonderful. If I have one or two volunteers at the same time, that would be ideal. However, having 4-6 volunteers at the same time can be difficult. There are a few requirements before parents can volunteer in the classroom. These include the following procedures:

- Fill out the volunteer forms.

- Take a TB skin test.

- Notify me at least one day in advance after you have filed your volunteer papers.

(continued)

FIGURE 4.44. Continued

Student's Section: The following selected pieces of work are the students' original work. They have not been edited. It will give you an idea of how our first-grade students are progressing.

A Story Written by Laura Thornton:

Staefesh er bloo. And starfesh er red. And Stasfesh ckan hid to. And sterfesh er beg. And sterfesh lev in the se. And sterfesh swem. And sterfesh er slao.

A Story Rewritten With the Help of the Teacher:

Starfish are blue and red. They hide in rocks. Some are big and some are small. They live in the sea. Starfish swim slowly in the sea.

A Story Written by Amanda Stamps:

Hokey is kind of hard. It takes practice. You have to try roller blades first or else you will not no how to skate. You need a puc. And a hokey stick and gear. And then you could play.

A Story Rewritten With the Help of the Teacher:

Hockey is kind of hard. It takes practice. You have to try roller blades if you want to know how to skate. You need a puck and gear and a hockey stick. You also need a helmet.

Parent's Section:

This section of the newsletter is dedicated for parent submissions. If you have any you would like to publish in our upcoming classroom newsletter, please submit your communications each month by the 15th. This newsletter section will allow you to communicate with all of the parents in the classroom. If you are looking for a baby-sitter, have messages to communicate, or need suggestions on how to help your child, this section will provide the opportunity for you to communicate with parents in similar situations.

FIGURE 4.45. Sample Student Observation Form for Volunteer Usage

Observe one student other than your own child in the classroom for 10 minutes, and answer the following questions:

Describe the activity that the observed student is doing.

What is the student saying, and what are his or her actions during the activity?

What emotions is the student displaying while working with this activity? Does the student appear happy, frustrated, bored, or sad?

Did the teacher, the aide, or a volunteer talk with the student during this observation? If there was an interaction, describe the conversation and how the student responded to the adult.

Describe what you learned by watching this student for 10 minutes.

How can you use this observation technique at home when helping your child with his or her schoolwork?

FIGURE 4.46. Part 8 Overhead for Workshop Group Activity

Identifying Strategies for Peer Mentoring Opportunities Using Parent and Community Volunteers in the Classroom

Identify ways volunteers can support each other in the classroom through peer mentoring:

1.

2.

3.

4.

5.

6.

7.

8.

9.

10.

11.

12.

FIGURE 4.47. Part 8 Overhead for Workshop Training

Identifying Strategies for Peer Mentoring Opportunities Using Parent and Community Volunteers in the Classroom

Parent and community volunteers can provide each other with peer mentoring support in the following ways:

❑ Parents can assist community volunteers in understanding the unique learning needs of their school community's children.

❑ Parents can help community volunteers understand the cultural differences of their school community's children.

❑ Parents can help community volunteers understand age-appropriate classroom management strategies.

❑ Parents can model effective strategies for helping community volunteers support the students' learning needs based on their own success in helping their children with their homework.

❑ Parents can share their cultural experiences in program planning and providing enrichment experiences for students with community volunteers.

❑ Community volunteers can provide language support to parents who are not fluent in English.

❑ Community volunteers can help parents learn more about other resources available to families in their community.

❑ Community volunteers can bring career and community resources to the classroom for educational enrichment experiences for students and their parents.

❑ Community volunteers can provide career support to parents who are interested in exploring other career paths.

❑ Community volunteers can partner with parents in program planning and in providing supplementary community experiences for enrichment activities.

❑ Limited-English-speaking parent volunteers partnered with English-speaking community volunteers can provide the best combination of support to multilingual classrooms in overcoming any language barriers that might occur (Burke, 1999).

FIGURE 4.48. Part 9 Overhead for Workshop Group Activity

Sharing a Volunteer's Cultural Experiences
for Program Planning

Partner with a colleague, and brainstorm strategies for using volunteers to support cultural experiences in your program planning:

1.

2.

3.

4.

5.

6.

7.

8.

9.

10.

11.

12.

FIGURE 4.49. Part 9 Overhead for Workshop Training

Sharing a Volunteer's Cultural Experiences for Program Planning

When most children start school, they are seen as competent in their own homes and neighborhoods (Perkins, 1995). How the context of a child's early learning experiences is perceived by a teacher can have a significant impact on a child's academic performance in the classroom (WestEd, 1996). When a student's cultural experiences are viewed with respect, students will take the risks required for learning new concepts.

To achieve respect for students' diversity, teachers must incorporate content materials that refer to the students' interests, concerns, and issues of their home and community (WestEd, 1996). Parent and community volunteers can support teachers in their program planning through the following activities:

❑ Holiday celebrations can provide opportunities to research the event through culturally sensitive books and enrichment activities.

❑ Classroom volunteers can organize units of study that explore the various roles of different community members from diverse cultures.

❑ Classroom volunteers can organize holiday enrichment activities that include meals, crafts, a performance, writing a book about an event, visiting a cultural event, and having guest speakers.

❑ Classroom volunteers can organize a cultural fair.

❑ Classroom volunteers can create a multicultural book about each student's heritage with a family tree.

❑ Monthly family programs and potluck events can be organized by volunteers that are centered on different cultural themes.

All literacy activities involve life and literature. When teachers take the opportunity to partner with parents and expand the parents' education along with that of their children, the students have a greater opportunity for academic success (Perkins, 1995).

FIGURE 4.50. Part 10 Overhead for Workshop Group Activity

Volunteer Career Development and Cross-Training for Additional School Volunteer Opportunities

In small groups, create a list of training topics for a volunteer's career development, and list cross-training opportunities for a volunteer to support other school functions:

1.

2.

3.

4.

5.

6.

7.

8.

9.

10.

11.

12.

FIGURE 4.51. Part 10 Overhead for Workshop Training

Volunteer Career Development and Cross-Training for Additional School Volunteer Opportunities

Parent and community volunteers need ongoing training, career assessment, support, and opportunities to support the school in other functions. How a teacher and the school respond to its volunteers' professional development and personal growth needs is critical for the ongoing growth of a school's volunteer program. Schools should consider having monthly professional development meetings and sending volunteers to relevant conferences to support these professional growth needs. The following is a list of topics that can support volunteers in their career development:

❑ Effective communication skill development

❑ Cultural diversity education

❑ Conflict resolution techniques

❑ Self-esteem strategies for success

❑ Stress management strategies

❑ Career evaluation and guidance

❑ Leadership development

(continued)

FIGURE 4.51. Continued

The school staff should also consider other functional and leadership opportunities that parents and volunteers can train for and be promoted to. Research has indicated that parents and community members become more committed to serving schools as they become more aware of the needs of schools and how they can serve those needs (Burke, 1999). The following is a list of possible roles that volunteers can serve with proper supervision, resources, and training within a school:

❑ Parents can assist with the development of schoolwide family literacy programs.

❑ Parents can partner with community agencies in organizing social service family centers that can provide health services, basic needs services, mental health services, legal aid referrals, job training, career guidance, and child care.

❑ Parent and community volunteers can assist schools in building community and business partnerships for community problem solving and resource development.

❑ Parent and community volunteers can assist schools in writing grants and building collaborative relationships for fund development.

❑ Parent and community volunteers can organize community education forums about community safety issues, literacy and job development opportunities, strategic and facility planning, and election information.

❑ Parent and community volunteers can assist schools in building comprehensive job development and child care programs.

❑ Parent and community volunteers can network with local businesses in securing computers and computer literacy skills to support every child in their daily classroom work and future workforce development.

In addition to providing parent and community volunteers with career development and cross-training, the school should provide monthly volunteer recognition events that include:

❑ Ceremonial events or school assemblies in which volunteers receive plaques, certificates, pins, gifts, and privileges for accomplishments and for length of service (Burke & Liljenstolpe, 1992)

❑ Special recognition dinners with community entertainment, gifts, and proclamations from public officials

❑ Opportunities to speak on behalf of the school at community meetings and at conferences about their experiences as a school volunteer

❑ Opportunities to serve as a community volunteer on education and community commissions, advisory groups, and governmental meetings

FIGURE 4.52. Posttraining Evaluation on How to Use Parents and Volunteers in the Classroom

Consider the following statements as they relate to your usage of volunteers in the classroom, and circle the appropriate numerical value for each:

	High				**Low**
1. Parent participation for students is important.	1	2	3	4	5
2. Classroom participation for parents contributes to students' academic success.	1	2	3	4	5
3. Recruiting community volunteers to support students' academic achievement is important.	1	2	3	4	5
4. It is important to include community volunteers at the school to increase the community's understanding about the school.	1	2	3	4	5
5. I can work with up to four volunteers a day to support students' literacy skills.	1	2	3	4	5
6. I am not confident working with classroom volunteers.	1	2	3	4	5
7. Most community tutoring programs are fragmented.	1	2	3	4	5
8. Illiterate parent and community volunteers provide limited academic support services.	1	2	3	4	5
9. I can identify at least four parent or community volunteers who would be helpful as classroom tutors or mentors.	1	2	3	4	5
10. I am confident recruiting parents and community volunteers.	1	2	3	4	5
11. I am confident about using volunteers in my classroom.	1	2	3	4	5
12. Managing and training volunteers is challenging.	1	2	3	4	5

Volunteer Strategies to Support Literacy Activities

Volunteer strategies for supporting students' literacy activities can vary within a school. In addition to having parent and community volunteers support students in the classroom, schools can create breakfast family literacy activities, after-school homework clubs, and evening or weekend family literacy programs. Multigenerational family literacy programs can build on a family's strengths. These programs are designed to provide the tools and support a family needs to become stronger and more self-sufficient (National Center for Family Literacy, 1998a). A school-based family literacy program can include the following activities:

- Shared meals with a story time and literacy activities

- Academic enrichment preschool classes for toddlers

- Parent and child small group literacy skill-building activities

- A parent literacy program in an adult classroom on basic educational skills

- Parent education and training sessions on child development and study skills

- Job shadowing and opportunities for volunteering in a structured work environment to reinforce a parent's literacy development

- Home visits to reinforce family literacy

Creating a Family Literacy Program

To create a family literacy program, the school must first assess the educational and noneducational needs of its school and community families to identify gaps in literacy services available in the community (National Center for Family Literacy, 1998b). Learning about the needs of various cultural groups in the school community is essential for developing an appropriate literacy program. On the basis of this needs assessment, the school can identify appropriate goals, objectives, and outcomes for program participants and determine how it will measure these outcomes. For example, goals for adult learners can include exposure to a variety of children's books that will build confidence in the learner and increase his or her proficiency in reading, writing, and discussion (Goldsmith & Handel, 1990). Goals for other family members can include fostering a healthy, academic supportive relationship between adult family members and children while increasing the number of books available in the home.

Local community-based organizations should be contacted to provide added program support. Program staffing must include teachers who have a background in literacy development for different age groups and staff who have training in working with the school community's cultures. Once the program is designed, community volunteers can be recruited and trained to support the various family literacy program components. The following sections provide a summary of academic activities that can be used by trained volunteers and parents to support students' skill development in reading, language arts, math, science, social studies, computers, and the performing arts.

Reading

The knowledge that reading offers enjoyment and opportunities for learning provides students and their families with a basic understanding of why reading is important. There are four types of cueing systems to read for meaning. Students must consider their prior knowledge, how that knowledge relates to the meanings of words in a specific context, the function of words to convey meaning, and how the letters relate to the sounds in words (Perkins, 1995). Parents and volunteers can support students' reading achievement by using the following strategies:

- Prepare the student for reading the passage, pause and allow the student to identify a meaning within the context of the passage, prompt by asking questions about meaning, praise efforts, and probe by asking clarifying questions to reinforce comprehension.

- Help students learn how to use a table of contents, a dictionary, an encyclopedia, and other reference materials to further develop literacy skills.

- Study the text, illustrations and headings, and predict what the story is about.

- Provide background information about the story, and research various concepts introduced in the story on the Internet or through a library research project.

- Study each character's development, the setting of the story, the point of view of the author, the mood, the tone, the type of story, and the type of dialogue used in the story.

- Use holidays and traditions to expand a student's contextual and cultural understanding of a story.

- Link any indicators of what the story is about to prior learning and experiences.

- Continue through a difficult passage, and try to link the difficult parts to meaningful language.

- Ask clarification, comprehension, and prediction questions to increase understanding.

- Use the five senses, and incorporate auditory, visual, and kinesthetic learning strategies to increase comprehension.

- Create comprehension worksheets that include drawing, participating in an activity, or creating an art experience to increase understanding.

- Review unknown sections of the text, and clarify by connecting to known concepts.

Writing

Writing should be encouraged with spelling approximations. When parents learn to cherish creative spelling, students will significantly increase the amount of time they engage in productive and creative writing activities (Perkins, 1995). The following list includes diverse opportunities for parent and community volunteers to encourage students' written expression:

- Help students develop effective writing skills by teaching them how to write a descriptive passage, a narrative story about a personal experience, an informative article with instructions, a persuasive article presenting their point of view, or a report on a topic of interest.

- Writing opportunities to further develop skills include designing advertisements, bumper sticker slogans, fortunes, tongue twisters, greeting cards, jingles, and song lyrics.

- Create story maps to organize thoughts for writing.

- Create a game of having students identify proper verb usage by telling a story and having them identify verbs throughout the story to increase their understanding of word usage.

Math

Developing an understanding of mathematical concepts is part of daily life. Parent and community volunteers can help students improve their mathematical abilities by engaging them in the following activities:

- Play a tapping game, in which you have the student count mentally how many times you tapped and tell you the total number of one sequence of taps and the total of multiple sequences of taps.

- Help students create recipes using foods they like to eat.

- Help students identify patterns in the classroom, in food, on their clothes, and in outside objects.

- Drill students on their addition, subtraction, multiplication, and division math facts.

- Help students make change and compare prices of similar items.

- Assist students with learning how to tell time in various parts of the world.

- Measure the size of various objects in the classroom, and identify the geometric shapes and patterns contained within these objects.

- Help students create a model of various objects by breaking the objects into various geometric shapes. Students can also design a scale legend for constructing the object in a different size.

- Have students create a journal of their height and weight measurements over time and the distances they walk to various destinations.

Science

Science is the study of the facts and interaction of everything around us. How we understand the material world is defined through scientific methods. The following list describes creative approaches for assisting students in scientific exploration:

- Help students explore nature by going on nature walks to observe different trees, plants, flowers, insects, birds, animals, rocks, and other natural resources.

- Help students create collections of various nature items and write an observational report on the differences of various groupings.

- Help students create science experiments and compare the results of similar experiments.

- Help students observe, identify, categorize, and compare similarities and differences of household object collections.

- Study and compare various parts of the human body and the planets in the solar system.

Social Studies

The United States is a nation of immigrants. As travelers in an increasing mobile world, it is important to understand the rich cultural diversity within communities. Although some ancestors came to this country several generations ago, recent immigrants must have the opportunity to contribute the richness of their culture in various classroom activities (Perkins, 1995). The following activities will assist teachers in valuing the diversity of their students' cultures:

■ Discuss students' vacation destinations, and indicate their locations on a map.

■ Help students write stories about the types of companies and businesses for which their parents work in their community.

■ Use local, state, and country maps to help students identify rivers, oceans, mountain ranges, deserts, towns, cities, highways, roads, and major cities.

■ Use maps to help students write directions to various locations. Students can learn how to read the mileage legends on maps to identify how long it will take and the mileage required to reach a destination.

■ Help students create maps of their communities and identify where they live on the map.

■ Assist students with researching various community holidays and their community's history.

■ Help students create a family tree of their ancestors and identify the countries from which each ancestor came.

■ Have students create family history journals about family traditions and cultural customs.

■ Help students research the countries from which their ancestors immigrated and mark these countries on a world map in the classroom.

Computers

Eighty percent of the American public believes that teaching students computer skills is essential and that students should have access to the Internet. Technology literacy includes the student's acquisition of computer skills for improved learning, productivity, and performance. Although technology usage seldom causes substantial changes in schools, it can play a significant role in student achievement when it is appropriately introduced, applied, and used (Otterbourg, n.d.). Computer software programs allow students to create written materials more efficiently, graph statistical data, and create artistic materials. Becoming computer literate is critical for future job placement and development. Parent and community volunteers can assist students in developing their computer literacy skills through the following activities:

■ Help students play various reading, math, and language arts skill-building computer games.

- Help students write and edit stories by mastering basic word processing software.

- Teach students how to graphically illustrate and design greeting cards and pamphlets using graphic software.

- Assist students in organizing mathematical data using various graphing software applications.

- Assist students in collecting, organizing, and analyzing scientific data using various graphical and organizational database software applications.

- Assist students in creating music, songs, and artistic designs using performing arts software applications.

- Help students and their parents understand how to mange various household tasks using software programs.

- Help students learn how to research various topics on the Internet.

- Help students store their computer project data in their own computer data files.

- Help students learn how to create software programs and application procedures to support their academic subject areas.

Performing Arts

Performing arts experiences provide students with opportunities to creatively express themselves and their cultures through singing, dancing, and art projects. Parents and community volunteers can support students in their performing arts development through the following activities:

- Help students create culturally diverse performances with an introduction to basic acting, voice instruction, dance, casting techniques, set and costume design, stage development, and choreography.

- Teach students the basic principles of music by using a recorder.

- Listen to a wide variety of music to help students identify different instruments and develop an appreciation of culturally diverse composers and different types of music.

- Assist students in creating their own percussion instruments using inexpensive household items.

- Provide art materials for students to use to design and create art projects.

Building Community Collaborations for Added Resources

6

Thirty years of research indicates that greater family involvement in student's learning is a critical link to achieving high-quality education and a safe, disciplined environment to enhance academic achievement (U.S. Department of Education, 1994). In addition to participating in the classroom, families can join community volunteers, agencies, and businesses in establishing community partnerships that ensure:

- Safe and secure schools

- Learning that is viewed as important by all stakeholders

- Parent training and school-linked community services to support student achievement

- Increased resources for the school

- The effective use of coordinated and integrated support services at the school

The use of school-based community resources can include offering community enrichment programs, having community mentors support students, providing health and human care services, and receiving local business support (U.S. Department of Education, 1994). For example, the acquisition of technology literacy requires costly and complex support services. Through their wealth of practical experiences in using technology, businesses can support technology needs at schools (Otterbourg, n.d.). Businesses can also create strategic education alliances that meet local industry needs and promote systemic educational change (Ballen, Casey, & de Kanter, 1998).

A school's practices to encourage parents to participate in their children's education are vital for academic success. Effective school partnership practices that nurture parent and community involvement include mutual respect, trust, an ongoing exchange of information, and school and community problem-solving meetings that include defined roles and responsibilities for the various stake-holders (U.S. Department of Education, 1994). When schools create family and community resource centers, they demonstrate by their actions that parents and community volunteers are vital for supporting students' academic success. Community problem-solving efforts at schools have accomplished the following (U.S. Department of Education, 1994; Batey, 1996; Schmitt & Tracy, 1996; Ballen et al., 1998; Burke, 1999):

- Reduced alcohol usage, drug usage, and incidents of violence at school

- Challenged racism and promoted racial justice and equity in education

- Reinforced effective child-rearing practices and the development of effective study skills

- Created schoolwide parent and community tutoring and mentoring programs

- Implemented business programs that promote parent and employee participation in education

- Created reflective service learning projects that integrate academic learning with collaborative service delivery in the community

- Created after-school, weekend, evening, and extended school-year programs

- Developed school-to-work initiatives

- Linked social services and business services at the school site

- Developed effective parent and community leaders at the school

- Made schoolwide wish lists to leverage community resources

- Contributed resources to schools, including accounting support, financial management, management development, and technological services

- Organized groups of parents for site-based decision making, educational reform advocacy, and advisory efforts

To facilitate a community problem-solving process, the school must seek out its parent and community leaders and build a culture of conversation. At an initial community problem-solving meeting, the school's stakeholders should define their vision of what they want to achieve and brainstorm strategies for achieving their vision. After the initial meeting, a planning subcommittee of stakeholders should meet to review the brainstorming notes and identify themes for possible program development. Once key themes are identified, the planning subcommittee can invite other relevant community organizations or leaders to future meetings. At follow-up community problem-solving meetings, priorities should be determined, and a strategic plan with measurable outcomes should be created (Melaville, 1999).

Seeking Funding

Once the strategic plan has been created, fundraising strategies for program sustainability must be considered. Funding options include leveraging existing services from community agencies and businesses, writing grants to government and private foundations, organizing ongoing fundraising events, obtaining sponsorships, and building communitywide capacity for services. The program's outcomes and impact on various stakeholder groups should continuously be evaluated after the program receives initial funding (Ballen et al., 1998).

Seeking grant funding requires the initial identification of funding options through Internet searches of federal, state, county, local, and private foundation funders. Internet Web sites that provide comprehensive grant-funding information include Fundnet, Grantmaker Information, Council on Foundations, Philanthropy News Digest, and The Internet Prospector. Community foundations and nonprofit resource centers provide fundraising resource libraries and referrals to agencies that provide fundraising support services. The Foundation Center in New York publishes fundraising directories and grant-writing books. The *Chronicle of Philanthropy,* published in Washington, D.C., is a periodical that provides updated grant funding and development information. Other funding newspapers and newsletters include the *Nonprofit Times, CD Publications,* and the *Nonprofit World Magazine.* A membership with the National Association of Fundraising Executives includes a subscription to *Philanthropy Today.*

Once a list of prospective funders has been identified, contact each funder to order funding guidelines and annual reports detailing previously funded projects. Funding guidelines will include specific limitations on the type of programs that will be considered for funding, the geographical locations for funding, the timeline for submitting grant applications, and the required information that must be included in a grant application (Burke & Liljenstolpe, 1993). Typical grant proposals include the information discussed in the following sections.

Introduction and Demographic Description

Your school's and community's demographic profile can provide the funder with a basic understanding about your school's and community's needs and characteristics. Statistical information that can be collected and reported includes the school's enrollment data, attendance and drop-out rates, the ethnic composition of the school community, the socioeconomic characteristics of students, the incidence of school crime, the number of English learners, the number of students living in foster care, the number of students requiring special education or counseling services, and the overall needs of the community.

Problem or Need Statement

The grant's problem or need statement is a detailed and documented description of the problem being addressed. It establishes the significance of the problem and the contribution of the proposed problem resolution. The needs statement links the problem and the proposed program solution to previous and existing research and program practices. Needs statements should include why a particular need requires immediate attention and identify other groups that are currently responding to this need (Hall, 1988).

Goals and Objectives

A goal provides a broad statement indicating the overall intent for the project. Objectives are specific and concrete statements that include defined timelines and measurable outcomes. A program goal may be to develop a parent training program for assisting teachers in the classroom. An objective to support this goal may state that 50% of the 25 parents who received volunteer training demonstrated adequate classroom support strategies at least 70% of the time. A proposed project should include all program goals and measurable objectives with a work plan of supporting activities and timelines.

Evaluation Plan

The grant evaluation plan should include adequate and appropriate evaluation instruments that will measure program objectives and outcomes. To measure volunteers' performance in the classroom, evaluation instruments can include a survey of classroom behaviors completed by the teacher. Focus groups of trained volunteers can provide further information about the survey results. Other evaluation instruments include in-depth interviews of program participants, comparisons of academic performance and attendance data during the project, comparisons of pre- and post-program knowledge and attitudinal surveys, journal observations, and rubrics for evaluating observations.

Staffing Qualifications and the School's Program Capacity

The qualifications of key program staff and the school's capacity for delivering program services are critical for program success. If the staff or school has prior experience working successfully with the targeted population in responding to the need, the funder will be confident that the program will be effectively implemented. A school's previous program experience with similar targeted populations can also assure funders of successful program outcomes.

Future Funding Plans

A proposed project must have a comprehensive plan for continuous funding to ensure a program's sustainability. Funding options include matching funding from other grants, program service fees, leveraging funding from local community agencies and businesses, corporate sponsorships, and event fundraising. Short- and long-term funding strategies should be included in the program plan.

Budget and Budget Narrative

The grant budget should include all program expenses for staffing, materials, supplies, space, equipment, travel, training, consultants, evaluation, and administrative overhead costs. Most funders limit the percentage of administrative overhead costs that can be requested for funding. The budget should also include all sources of requested and matching funds from grants, program service fees, fundraising events, and other types of donated funding. A detailed budget narrative will reflect the actual funding costs for each employee including benefits and a breakdown of all expenditures for the program.

Attachments

Grant attachments can include a school's published accountability report, audits, resumes of key project staff, letters of support, memorandums of understanding describing services to be provided by community partners, and other school reports.

The following steps will assist you in completing the grant development process and in effectively implementing your newly funded program:

1. Define the project or solution to the problem.

2. Identify how you will locate various funding sources.

3. Research prospective funders, and determine who may fund your proposed project.

4. Contact prospective funders, and request their annual report, grant solicitation guidelines, and any other publications.

5. Contact prospective funding partners or matching funders to coordinate the project development.

6. Research the project's need and various proposed program components by contacting organizations that are currently receiving program funding from prospective funders. Visit successful project sites, and collect reports that document the need for the project with effective problem-solving strategies and evaluation plans.

7. Create a grant proposal that includes all required grant components.

8. Mail the completed grant proposal, and follow-up on the grant's status using the funder's grant-funding timeline.

9. Once funded, contact all program funders and stakeholders to create a plan for successful program implementation.

10. If you need to change your work plan or the usage of your funding allocation, contact the funder to obtain permission for making program changes.

Schools as Economic Solutions to Communities

■ ■

Schools have evolved into complex institutions serving various purposes (Burke, 1999). Students view schools as places to learn and to socialize with other students. Parents view schools as learning institutions that provide their children with the skills necessary to become productive citizens and to contribute to their community's economy. Community members and businesses believe schools serve as a critical link to preparing students for futures in the community's workplace. Interest groups envision schools as instruments for achieving the larger social goal of economic development (Inger, 1990). Within inner-city communities, it is becoming increasingly difficult to educate students who are worried about how they and their families will survive. Some of today's inner-city schools provide educational services to a majority of students who live in foster care or who do not live with a biological parent. Most of these students struggle with feelings of hurt, abandonment, and anger. Getting to school is often a struggle for these students. Once they are at school, many of these children have little motivation for learning.

Schools and Economic Development

Schools can aid local economies through their community-based school-linked services and by making schooling a production function. Schools develop local economies through their linkages with the community and through their policies and procedures that encourage students and their families to increase their investment in learning (Kerchner, 1997). By empowering the community's stakeholders to support school-based community services and to provide academic support to students, the school acts as a powerful labor market intermediary. Through its various student and family programs, the school can regulate the flow of students and their family members, and community volunteers to employment opportunities within the community. Schools become creators of their community's economic development by providing the following economic services (Kerchner, 1997; Spring, 1998):

- Through their service delivery system, community-empowered schools can act as a community's asset-based indicator.

- Schools can disarm neighborhood crime and become a center for community pride.

- Community-empowered schools can model an effective democratic governance that allows all stakeholders to have an active voice in the school's decision-making process.

- Through their collaborative partnerships with community stakeholders, health care and social services agencies, and local businesses, community-empowered schools can become the engines of urban growth.

- Community-empowered schools have a moral obligation to develop learning outcomes for all culturally diverse students that can be defined at a specific cost.

There are many ways to measure whether or not educational programs provide a cost-effective approach to community economic development.

The Human Capital Approach

Through school-based community services, students can receive the social services support required to meet their basic needs. Schoolwide comprehensive parent and community volunteer programs can provide students with extended academic support services that are individualized to meet their unique learning needs. Although the school can somewhat compensate for the problems of living in an economically challenged area, Adler (1997) argues that the goal of a school—starting at the preschool level—must be to do whatever it takes to grow the middle class and shrink the underclass. Economists often call this *human capital development* (Burke, 1999).

Human capital can best be defined as the time, effort, and money spent on education to yield future returns on the investment. As with capital equipment, human capital is created by a production process often described through a production function (Baumol & Becker, 1996). The production function describes the outputs—measured in this case in terms of student learning—that result from allocation of physical resources, such as teachers and instructional materials. By developing the human capital of children, a community can reduce its dependency on government and private social services and increase the productivity of all community members. Schools provide an excellent way to offer all children equal access to the resources of the community. In these instances, human capital could be viewed as an integrated approach to economic and social development. The role of education then becomes defined as the contribution to a human's capacity to lead a worthwhile life, influence social change, and influence economic production (Sen, 1999).

When considering the value of training parents to become skilled teachers for their children and training community volunteers to provide added support services to families, it becomes clear that parents who receive training in language arts and academic skills can increase their own academic skills. These increased abilities can be correlated to increased job performance and income. A family literacy model of education for all of a school community's students will not only support the students' academic success but will also add to their community's overall academic and economic development (Burke, 1999).

Cost-Effectiveness as an Indicator

The community can provide a cost-effective resource to schools seeking to serve the diverse learning needs of economically challenged families. Conventional evaluation models for the measuring effectiveness of a program do not always capture the interactions among various outcomes that a strategy intends to achieve (Hayes, Lipoff, & Danegger, 1995). To address these concerns, a cost-benefit or cost-effectiveness analysis must be used as one part of a total evaluation process for selecting the most appropriate and cost-effective strategy.

A cost-effectiveness analysis of various approaches for linking community services to schools can be used to evaluate alternative solutions to a problem and to consider each solution's costs and effects with regard to producing some outcome or set of outcomes (Levin, 1983). The application of cost-effectiveness has an extensive history of use by the Bureau of Reclamation and the Army Corps of Engineers (Zebe & Dively, 1994). Although benefit-cost analysis is inherently biased in favor of quantifiable values, it can serve as an objective method for making decisions that must show benefits in excess of costs (Levin, 1983; Zebe & Dively, 1994).

These analytical tools are often complex and difficult to use. Moreover, individuals in local schools generally are not well trained in the use of production functions or cost-effectiveness analysis. Our purpose here is not to make you an expert in using such tools. We only want to point out that measuring the value of parent and community volunteer programs may provide additional benefits besides improved student achievement. The enhanced learning of both students and other community members may have a significant, long-term impact on the willingness of businesses to locate in your area (or to decide not to move from your area), leading to enhanced economic opportunities for your students and their families.

The Future of Community-Empowered Schools

■ ■

As community-empowered schools formulate systems of governance to support partnerships with parents, community volunteers, community organizations, and businesses, student achievement will improve and the links between families and schools will be strengthened (U.S. Department of Education, 1994). The first seven chapters of this book focused on how schools can become the hub of a community by creating governance structures, policies, and procedures that open the school's classrooms for interactive parent and community involvement. Chapter 4 provided a comprehensive training program for teachers on how to create a culturally sensitive parent and community volunteer program to support students' academic achievement. The research evidence contained in this book consistently emphasizes the value to students and their families in building effective school and community partnerships. When culturally diverse families are trained to help their children succeed in school, the families must fully participate in the process to internalize the change. Parents must learn new behaviors and language to support their child's learning. They must construct this new knowledge and awareness about their role in their child's education with their child's classroom teacher and the school's administrative staff (Delgado-Gaitan, 1990).

By examining multicultural and human rights education, students can select values that contribute to their human happiness and reduce economic inequalities among various groups (Spring, 1998). Social institutions can contribute to a school community's development by enhancing individual freedoms and sustaining the social commitment to help stabilize this effort (Sen, 1999). As schools expand their influence in the community and their governance structures to embrace more comprehensive community collaborations, they will continue to have an active voice in their community's economic development. Community-empowered schools have the potential to become fully integrated service systems with health and mental health services, early childhood education programs, an adult education learning center, a vocational education lab, supplemental academic enrichment courses, family recreational programs, and economic development services (Schmitt & Tracy, 1996).

To support these changes, school districts can provide technical support services to facilitate the school's independent governance, fundraising activities, and program development. A planned and integrated service delivery system requires visionary leadership at each school site and the design of a school site strategic plan to facilitate this process. This process for change begins with the school district's mission statement. The statement includes a commitment to community partnerships through policy boards and district leadership (Schmitt & Tracy, 1996). After a school completes its strategic plan and identifies appropriate resources to support programs, the school can leverage the human and financial resources required to put its plan into action.

The structure of the community-empowered school can include innovative configurations. In addition to the district's administrative and support services and early childhood programs, a school can offer a fundamental education program that includes significant service-learning work experience and mentoring from a community volunteer (Dodd, 1992). Community educational, recreational, and cultural activities can be available for all community stakeholders.

To support a school district's aggressive program for community empowerment and economic development, the community's local governance members and school stakeholders must seize the opportunity to raise the benchmark for supporting each student's unique learning style.

References

■ ■

Ada, A. F. (1988). The Pajaro Valley experience: Working with Spanish-speaking parents to develop children's reading and writing skills through the use of children's literature. In T. Skutnabb-Kangas & J. Cummins (Eds.), *Minority education: From shame to struggle* (pp. 223-237). Clevedon, UK: Multilingual Matters.

Adler, L. (1997). A proactive role for educators in local economic development: Shaping the future. *Education and Urban Society, 29*(4), 524-547.

Aronson, M. M. (1995). *Building communication partnerships with parents.* Westminster, CA: Teacher Created Materials.

Ballen, J., Casey, J. C., & de Kanter, A. (1998). *The corporate imperative: Results and benefits of business involvement in education.* Washington, DC: U.S. Department of Education.

Batey, C. S. (1996). *Parents are lifesavers: A handbook for parent involvement in schools.* Thousand Oaks, CA: Corwin Press.

Baumol, W. J., & Becker, W. E. (1996). The economist's approaches. In W. J. Baumol & W. E. Becker (Eds.), *Assessing educational practices: The contribution of economics* (pp. 1-16). Cambridge: MIT Press.

Burke, M. A. (1999). Analyzing the cost effectiveness of using parents and community volunteers to improve students' language arts test scores (Doctoral dissertation, University of Southern California, 1999). *Dissertation Abstracts International, A60/06,* Z1915.

Burke, M. A., & Liljenstolpe, C. (1992). *Recruiting volunteers: A guide for nonprofits.* Menlo Park, CA: Crisp.

Burke, M. A., & Liljenstolpe, C. (1993). *Creative fund-raising: A guide for success.* Menlo Park, CA: Crisp.

Delgado-Gaitan, C. (1990). *Literacy for empowerment: The role of parents in children's education.* Briston, PA: Falmer/Taylor & Francis.

Dodd, A. W. (1992). *A parent's guide to innovative education: Working with teachers, schools, and your children for real learning.* Chicago: Noble Press.

Epstein, J. L., Coates, L., Salinas, K. C., Sanders, M. G., & Simon, B. S. (1997). *School, family, and community partnerships: Your handbook for action.* Thousand Oaks, CA: Corwin Press.

Far West Laboratory. (1992). *How families teach, support, learn, make decisions.* San Francisco: Author. (ERIC Document Reproduction Service No. ED 344 962)

Funkhouser, J. E., Gonzales, M. R., & Moles, O. C. (1998). *Family involvement in children's education: Successful local approaches.* Washington, DC: Government Printing Office.

Goldsmith, E., & Handel, R. D. (1990). *Family reading: An intergenerational approach to literacy.* Syracuse, NY: New Readers Press, Division of Laubach Literacy International.

Hall, M. S. (1988). *Getting funded: A complete guide to proposal writing.* Portland, OR: Continuing Education.

Hayes, C. D., Lipoff, E., & Danegger, A. E. (1995). *Compendium of comprehensive, community-based initiatives.* Washington, DC: The Finance Project.

Henderson, A. T., & Berla, N. (1994). *A new generation of evidence: The family is critical to student achievement.* Washington, DC: National Committee for Citizens in Education.

Henderson, A. T., Marburger, C. L., & Ooms, T. (1986). *Beyond the bake sale: An educator's guide to working with parents.* Washington, DC: National Committee for Citizens in Education.

Inger, M. (1990). Community-based strategies for work-related education. *NCEE Brief, 10,* 1-4.

Karnes, M. B. (1979). The use of volunteers and parents in mainstreaming. *Viewpoints in Teaching and Learning, 55*(3), 44-56.

Kerchner, C. T. (1997). Education as a city's big industry. *Education and Urban Society, 29*(4), 424-441.

Klass, C. S., Pettinelli, J. D., & Wilson, M. (1993). Home visiting: Building a bridge between home and school. *Equity and Choice, 10* (1), 52-56.

Levin, H. M. (1983). *Cost-Effectiveness: A primer.* Beverly Hills, CA: Sage.

Lewis, A. (1992). Helping young urban parents educate themselves and their children. *ERIC/CUE Digest, 85,* 3-6.

McCaleb, S. P. (1994). *Building communities of learners.* Mahwah, NJ: Lawrence Erlbaum.

Melaville, T. (1999). *What works policy brief: Making a difference for children and families: The community approach.* Sacramento, CA: Foundation Consortium.

National Center for Family Literacy. (1998a). *Comprehensive family literacy programs change lives.* Louisville, KY: Author.

National Center for Family Literacy. (1998b). *How to begin a family literacy program.* Louisville, KY: Author.

Olsen, L., Chang, H., De La Rosa Salazar, D., Leong, C., McCall Perez, Z., McClain, G., & Raffel, L. (1994). *The unfinished journey: Restructuring schools in a diverse society.* San Francisco: California Tomorrow.

Otterbourg, S. D. (n.d.). *Corporate experiences: Using technology to strengthen employee and family involvement in education.* Washington, DC: U.S. Department of Education.

Perkins, P. (1995). *Family literacy: Parents as partners.* Westminster, CA: Teacher Created Materials.

Schmitt, D. M., & Tracy, J. C. (1996). *Gaining support for your school: Strategies for community involvement.* Thousand Oaks, CA: Corwin Press.

Sen, A. (1999). *Development as freedom.* New York: Knopf.

Short, P. M., & Greer, J. T. (1997). *Leadership in empowered schools.* Upper Saddle River, NJ: Prentice Hall.

Spring, J. (1998). *Education and the rise of the global economy.* Mahwah, NJ: Lawrence Erlbaum.

U.S. Department of Education. (1994). *Strong families, strong schools: Building community partnerships for learning.* Washington, DC: Author.

Valenzuela, A. (1999). *Subtractive schooling: U.S.-Mexican youth and the politics of caring.* Albany: State University of New York Press.

Violand-Sanchez, E., Sutton, C. P., & Ware, H. W. (1991). *Fostering home-school cooperation: Involving language minority families as partners in education.* Washington, DC: National Clearinghouse for Bilingual Education.

WestEd. (1996). *School reform: A new outlook.* San Francisco: Author.

White, B. L. (1987). Education begins at birth. *Principal, 66*(5), 15-17.

Young, T., & Westernoff, F. (1996). Overcoming barriers to effective parental partnerships: Implications for professionals in an educational setting. *Journal of Educational Issues for Language Minority Students* [On-line serial]. Available: http://www.ncbe.gwu.edu

Zebe, R. O., Jr., & Dively, D. D. (1994). *Benefit-cost analysis in theory and practice.* New York: HarperCollins.

Suggested Readings

Andrews, P. (1981). Parent involvement: A key to success. *Children Today, 10,* 21-23.

Becher, R. (1984). *Parent involvement: A review of research and principles of successful practices.* Washington, DC: National Institute of Education.

Beebe, M. K. (1976). Teachers and parents together. *Today's Education, 6,* 74-79.

Bernard, B. (1992). *Drug-free schools and communities, mentoring programs for urban youth: Handle with care.* Portland, OR: Northwest Regional Educational Laboratory.

Bronfenbrenner, U. (1974). *A report on longitudinal evaluations of preschool programs. Vol. 2: Is intervention effective?* Washington, DC: Government Printing Office.

Chavkin, N. F., Gonzalez, D. L., & Lara, D. (1995). Forging partnerships between Mexican American parents and the schools. *ERIC/CRESS Digest, 8,* 3-4.

Cloud, N., De Leon, T., Eugenio, J., Kimber, R. A., & Wu, S. T. (1989). *Multisystem system instructional planning for exceptional bilingual students.* New York: Institute for Urban and Minority Education.

Cronenwett, S., Vansickle, M., & Walker, F. (1996). *Mentoring handbook.* Sacramento: State of California Alcohol and Drug Programs, Resource Center Mentor Program.

Davis-Kennedy, P. (1996). *The effectiveness of parental involvement on reading achievement.* Chicago: Chicago Public Schools.

Delgado-Gaitan, C. (1991). Involving parents in the schools: A process of empowerment. *American Journal of Education, 100*(1), 20-46.

Far West Laboratory. (n.d.). *Parents and schools.* San Francisco: Author.

Grotberg, E. H. (1969). *Review of research 1965-1969.* Washington, DC: Government Printing Office.

Guthrie, L. F. (1989). *Educational partnerships in California: A survey of the California Educational Partnership Consortium.* San Francisco: Far West Laboratory.

Hartman, W. T., & Fay, T. A. (1996). Cost-effectiveness of instructional support teams in Pennsylvania. *Journal of Educational Finance, 21,* 555-580.

King, J. A. (1994). Meeting the educational needs of at-risk students: A cost analysis of three models. *Educational Evaluation and Policy Analysis, 16*(1), 1-19.

Langenbrunner, M. R., & Thornburg, K. R. (1980). Attitudes of preschool directors, teachers, and parents toward parent involvement in the schools. *Reading Improvement, 17*(4), 286-291.

Lankard, B. A. (1995). Business/education partnerships. *ERIC Digest, 156,* 1-4. (ERIC Document Reproduction Service No. ED 383 856)

Lazar, I. (1981). Early intervention is effective. *Educational Leadership, 38,* 303-305.

Lee, C. U. (1992). *A guide to evaluation strategies for mentoring programs and the mentoring center.* Berkeley: University of California, Institute of Urban and Regional Development.

The Mentoring Center. (1996). *Classification of mentoring relationship types.* Oakland, CA: Author.

Monk, D. H. (1993). *The cost of systemic education reform: Conceptual issues and preliminary estimates.* Unpublished manuscript.

Monk, D. H. (1995). The costs of pupil performance assessment: A summary report. *Journal of Education Finance, 20*(4), 363-371.

Monk, D. H. (1996). The importance of balance in the study of educational costs. *Journal of Education Finance, 21*(4), 590-591.

National Education Goals Panel. (1997). *The national education goals report.* Washington, DC: Author.

North Central Regional Education Laboratory. (1998). *School-family partnership: A literature review* [On-line]. Available: http://www.ncrel.org/sdrs/pidata/pi01trev.htm

Peters, D. (1978, March 24). Parents into the mainstream. *Times Educational Supplement,* p. 16.

Picus, L. O. (1994). *A conceptual framework for analyzing the costs of alternative assessment* (Tech. Rep. No. 384). Los Angeles: University of California, National Center for Research on Evaluation, Standards, and Student Teaching.

Picus, L. O., & Tralli, A. (1998). *Alternative assessment programs: What are the true costs? An analysis of the total cost of assessment in Kentucky and Vermont* (Tech. Rep. No. 441). Los Angeles: University of California, National Center for Research on Evaluation, Standards, and Student Teaching.

Radin, N. (1972). Three degrees of maternal involvement in a preschool program: Impact on mothers and children. *Child Development, 43,* 1355-1364.

Rebman, V. L. (1983). The effect of parental attitudes and program duration upon parental participation patterns in a pre-school education program. *Child Study Journal, 13*(1), 57-71.

Schaefer, E. S. (1972). Parents as educators: Evidence from cross-sectional, longitudinal, and intervention research. *Young Children, 27,* 227-239.

Scott, R. (1976). Home start: Third-grade follow-up assessment of a family-centered pre-school enrichment program. *Psychology in the Schools, 13,* 435-438.

State of California Governor's Office of Child Development and Education. (1998). *Academic volunteer and mentor service program annual report to the legislature fiscal year 1996-97.* Sacramento, CA: Author.

Truby, R. (1987). Home-school projects that work. *Education and Urban Society, 19*(2), 206-211.

Walberg, H. (1985). *A research report on parent involvement.* Alexandria, VA: National Community Education Association.

Warfield, M. E. (1994). A cost-effectiveness analysis of early intervention services in Massachusetts: Implications for policy. *Educational Evaluation and Policy Analysis, 16*(1), 87-99.

Whitmore, K. R. (1988). *The Rochester initiative.* Rochester, NY: Eastman Kodak.

Woodside, W. S. (1985). *Business in education: How good a grade? ERS concerns in education.* Arlington, VA: Educational Research Service.

Zebe, R. O., Jr. (1998). Is cost effectiveness legal? Three rules. *Journal of Policy Analysis and Management, 17*(3), 419-456.

Index